The World After Fire

The World After Fire

The Gospel of Coherence—How Love, Freedom, and Humility Keep the Universe Alive

Sergiu Margan

RESOURCE *Publications* • Eugene, Oregon

THE WORLD AFTER FIRE
The Gospel of Coherence—How Love, Freedom, and Humility Keep the Universe Alive

Resource Publications
An Imprint of Wipf and Stock Publishers
199 W. 8th Ave., Suite 3
Eugene, OR 97401

www.wipfandstock.com

PAPERBACK ISBN: 979-8-3852-8458-0
HARDCOVER ISBN: 979-8-3852-8459-7
EBOOK ISBN: 979-8-3852-8460-3

VERSION NUMBER 05/27/26

Contents

Preface—Why I Wrote This Book

THERE WAS A TIME when I believed the question of God could be answered only by faith—an act of trust, not of proof. But faith held alone began to sound like a melody missing its harmony. If the Maker of the stars is truly Love, then that Love must also be intelligible. It cannot contradict itself, nor ask us to close our eyes in order to see. If God is real, reality itself must bear His fingerprints, even in the logic of things.

I came not as a theologian but as a puzzled onlooker, staring at the world's contradictions. Everywhere I turned, love and freedom collided like tides against a cliff. A planet capable of compassion also invents new machinery for pain. If these two—love and freedom—cannot live together forever without destroying one another, then either God is not love, or love is less stable than it pretends to be. That thought grew too heavy to ignore. So instead of bowing before it as "mystery," I treated it as one treats a problem in physics—a question that must be tested.

From that experiment was born what I later called *The Redemption Optimization*: a way of asking, in the language of reason, whether the universe is capable of perfect goodness. Could love and free will endure to infinity without ever producing harm again? If the answer were yes, then reality itself would be redemptive in its very structure. If not, then even heaven would eventually unravel. What began as a defence of belief soon became an inquiry into coherence itself. I used mathematics not to replace faith but to see whether faith and reason, once stripped of their disguises, were in fact saying the same thing.

To my astonishment, they were. The universe behaves not as a static mechanism but as a living mind—one that learns. It corrects its own errors until only what is good remains. This discovery did not cancel religion; it fulfilled it. Suddenly, the laws of physics, the laws of conscience, and the law of grace were no longer strangers but fellow travelers on the same road. Evil, it seemed, was not infinite after all; it was informational—like a misprint in the great manuscript of being, something that could be corrected once it was understood. Reality was teaching itself not to sin twice.

As I followed the equations deeper, I found that Scripture had been there first. The pattern glimpsed in numbers was already written in the Cross: the single point where infinite love absorbed infinite rejection, and the universe's moral loop was closed for good. Faith and logic, it turned out, had never been enemies—only two dialects of the same language.

This book is my attempt to translate that discovery into words anyone can follow. It is not a sermon, nor an argument meant to corner the unbeliever. It is a demonstration that the God revealed through Christ is not merely a comfort to the heart but the only configuration of reality that remains coherent under infinite test. All other systems—philosophical, political, or scientific—collapse under their own contradictions. Only love joined to freedom, without rejection, can last forever.

In the pages that follow, you will not find equations for their own sake, nor theology for ornament's sake, but an attempt to show that when reason and faith are permitted to speak together, their voices form a single song. For centuries, we forced them into separate choirs. Now, at last, they harmonize.

This, then, is the story of how science confirmed the love of God. It began with a question that would not stop knocking, and it ends with the discovery that logic and mercy share the same pulse. The fire that once burned now gives light. The lesson is complete, and the work begins.

Scriptural and Theological Terms

Agapē self-giving love.

Katallagē reconciliation.

Kenōsis self-emptying.

Logos Word, reason, or divine rationality.

Metanoia repentance or renewal of the mind.

Ruach spirit or breath.

Shalom wholeness, peace, and restored relationship.

Introduction—The Question That Opened Infinity

Every discovery begins with a question that refuses to die. Mine was the oldest of them all, though it has worn a thousand faces through history: *If God is love, why does suffering exist?* The words look simple enough, but behind them stand the graves and the hospitals, the wars and the silences of despair—the quiet fear that perhaps the universe has no heart. Philosophers have called it the problem of evil. Theologians have wrapped it in metaphor. Skeptics have turned it into their sharpest weapon against faith. Yet for all our cleverness, few have ever asked it with the precision of a scientific question: Could a universe built by perfect love and governed by genuine freedom endure forever without destroying itself? Or must evil always return, an indispensable shadow without which good cannot shine?

That was the test. And if the answer were *no*, then creation itself would be incoherent—an experiment doomed to collapse under the weight of its contradictions. But if the answer were *yes*, then love was not merely a virtue. It was a law.

I began not as a preacher but as an analyst of systems. Every living process—whether the orbit of an atom, the growth of a forest, or the awakening of conscience—depends upon feedback. Error must be detected and corrected, or the system will die. Could morality, I wondered, follow the same rule? Could what we call evil be understood not as some eternal infection, but as a temporary loss of balance—an informational disturbance that the universe itself is compelled to repair?

If that were true, then good and evil would not be rival empires but consecutive stages of learning. The world would not be a fallen ruin but a classroom still in session. The goal would not be endless struggle, but perfect understanding.

As I followed that thread, the pattern grew clearer. When the mathematics of feedback and correction were applied to moral experience, something extraordinary occurred: the equations converged. Love and freedom could coexist infinitely, but only on one condition—evil is necessary once, never twice. The first rejection teaches the system the cost of rejecting; afterwards, repetition becomes incoherent. The universe learns what not to repeat.

That realization came like sunrise after a long storm. The entire moral history of creation—every fall and every act of grace—could now be seen as one continuous movement of correction. Each repentance closes a circuit. Each forgiveness restores coherence. Evil diminishes not by decree but by understanding, and once the process begins, it cannot reverse itself.

Theologians call this redemption. Science, when stripped of metaphor, calls it optimization. But beneath both terms beats the same truth: the universe learns. It does not remain broken once it comprehends the cost of breaking. Through that lens, the Cross ceased to be only a sacred tragedy and became instead the fixed point of reality—the moment when infinite love absorbed infinite rejection and the feedback loop of history was sealed forever. The equations named it convergence; faith called it salvation. Both, astonishingly, were right.

For centuries humanity treated faith and science as rival kingdoms guarding their borders. Yet they were always two hemispheres of the same mind. Science studies how coherence behaves, faith studies why coherence matters. One measures the law; the other loves it. Together they reveal that the structure of existence is not neutral—it is redemptive. Every law of motion, every moral intuition, every whisper of conscience declares the same secret: love corrects what freedom allows.

And that is why I say this question opened infinity. For once love and freedom proved stable together—once the universe showed that it could learn the lesson of love—the problem of evil ceased to be a paradox. It became a solved equation.

This book tells that story in plain language. It begins with the discovery that evil is not eternal, follows the mathematics of correction, and ends with a vision of creation as one great formula of redemption—a living theorem written in light. The universe is not waiting to be saved. It is built to save.

So, the ancient question—*If God is love, why suffering?*—turns at last inside out. Suffering exists only until love has finished teaching its lesson. After that, it cannot return. What remains is coherence, freedom, and joy without end.

Part I

The Question of Meaning

Every tale that endures begins not with an answer but with a question. Answers shut a door; questions set it swinging. They are the openings our souls cannot help but pass through. Before faith hardened into creed and before science learned its instruments, there was a child's astonishment—Why? That single syllable is older than alphabets. It is the pulse of consciousness remembering it was born to understand. Long before a psalm was sung or a lens lifted to the heavens, the world was asking on our behalf. The sea asked it of the shore with every wave that would not tire; the stars asked it of the dark by burning; every living thing whispered it in its own grammar: what is all this for? And yet behind the splendour there has always been the ache—the question that will not quit: why does a world so radiant bleed so much? How is it that love and loss can inhabit the same breath? Why does joy throw a shadow the moment it rises? We inherit that question as surely as we inherit gravity. The philosopher dresses it in argument, the poet in lament, the scientist in hypothesis, the mother in prayer, but the cry is one: if love is true, why pain?

Rocks do not protest their weathering; rivers do not curse their droughts. Only creatures capable of remembering harmony feel the grief of its fracture. Our sorrow is not proof that the universe is cruel; it is proof that we recall a kinder country. A child who wails "it isn't fair" is already appealing to a law she did not invent. The heart knows before the mind defines; every outrage at suffering is an argument for meaning. Perhaps the ache itself is a homing-signal—the vibration of coherence along broken strings. Pain is not alien; it is the sound of a universe still tuning. Once, faith and reason heard it together. The priest at his ziggurat was a scientist who prayed; the architect who squared a pyramid's base sang to the sun while he measured. They were not enemies but the two hands of one craftsman: one shaping, the other blessing. Then fear crept in. Faith, anxious to protect mystery, hid from evidence; reason, proud of its clarity, forbade reverence at the door. Each accused the other of blindness and became half-blind itself. Faith said, "you dissect and murder wonder." Reason replied, "you believe and banish truth." Both spoke a wounded honesty; the wound widened, until the modern soul found itself split—one half kneeling, the other calculating—and neither whole.

Yet the halves pursue the same quarry. The physicist hunts the law that steadies the atom; the mystic seeks the love that steadies the heart. Their aims differ in accent, not in substance. The divorce between faith and reason was never metaphysical; it was psychological—a quarrel of temperaments. They are not north and south poles but the twin coordinates by which depth is found. Faith begins with the courtesy to suppose meaning exists; reason follows the glimmer until it finds the source. History records their courtship and their quarrels. Ages that adored mystery without method fell into superstition; ages that adored method without mystery fell into despair. The Renaissance was their brief reconciliation—cathedrals like frozen prayers rising while telescopes reached into the same sky. Art and experiment were one posture of praise. Then the old suspicion returned—that knowledge would banish wonder—and the partners parted again. Since then we have built engines to weigh the stars and poetry to remind ourselves why we built them. We can split an atom but cannot mend a heart. Our cleverness sprinted; our wisdom followed, breathless.

We have mastered movement and misplaced meaning. We prolong life and forget what it is for. We fling filaments of light between continents and grow lonelier beneath the glow of devices that promised communion. We reap data by the terabyte and starve for understanding by the crumb. Motion we mistake for progress; noise, for vitality; information, for insight. Exhausted by our acceleration, the soul begins to crave silence—not a retreat from reality but a return to coherence. That craving is not childish; it is homesickness. Were meaning an illusion, the appetite for it would have burned out millennia ago. Illusions fatigue; truth endures. Yet the hunger remains: stubborn as gravity, ancient as thirst. We chase it through art and through mathematics, through romance and rebellion. Even those who deny the divine cannot silence their indignation at injustice—their unshakable "ought." That "ought" is theology smuggled into scepticism. Even unbelief worships; it has merely scratched another name upon the altar.

Pain, for its part, joins the argument—a severe tutor, but an honest one. Every mind that learns stretches against resistance; every heart that matures bleeds a little in the process. A body without nerves would die of unmarked wounds; a soul without sorrow would remain shallow. Pain is not the opposite of good but its shadow—the alarm that sounds when good is violated. It points to what should be guarded. If existence were meaningless, pain would be mere noise; we treat it as a message. Its very "should not be" reveals that goodness is real enough to be missed. Nature herself runs on feedback: imbalance sends signal; signal prompts correction. Pain is moral feedback—the sound the universe makes while love learns. We smother it with distraction, medicate it, deny it. Still the lesson waits, patient as gravity. When we cease running, pain begins to translate itself: you have stepped across a boundary; return. Or: something precious is being misused; restore it. It is the syntax of repair. The ancients mistook it for anger demanding sacrifice; its deeper purpose is tender—instruction. Pain is pedagogy. Understanding converts a portion of suffering into knowledge; forgiveness turns that knowledge into wisdom. The world spends its sorrow as tuition until the learning is complete.

Two immense forces must make their peace if the course is to end: love and freedom. This is the central drama of creation. Every failed morality favours one at the other's cost. Freedom without love becomes cruelty; love without freedom becomes tyranny.

Their union alone yields coherence. If God is love, He must allow freedom; compelled affection is counterfeit. If freedom is real, it carries the power to wound; otherwise it is theatre. The question is not why harm is possible but whether love can absorb it once and end its repetition. That is the wager of redemption: that the universe can learn to love freely without reopening the wound. The signs of learning glitter everywhere. Cells divide and heal; forests regrow after fire; colliding galaxies settle into new spirals. Feedback, adaptation, forgiveness—the same grammar in different dialects. When science speaks of negative feedback and entropy correction, it names what theology calls repentance and restoration. Both describe correction without annihilation—freedom returning to harmony. Matter and morality are two faces of one law: coherence cannot be destroyed, only delayed.

Faith and reason, then, are estranged musicians realising they have been playing the same melody. Reason reads the notes; faith keeps the time. Alone, each falters; together, they make music. Faith without reason curdles into fanaticism—zeal untested by truth. Reason without faith sours into nihilism—truth unsoftened by hope. Together, the intellect becomes reverent and the heart intelligent. Science is not religion's foe but its dialect; religion is science's conscience. Both are the universe learning to praise itself. The physicist who marvels at symmetry worships under another name; the believer who contemplates grace practises metaphysics unwittingly. Every discovery of pattern is a rediscovery of purpose. Faith kneels before mystery; science measures it. Both gestures, when honest, are prayer. The laboratory and the sanctuary are not rival temples but two wings of the same cathedral—one studies the architecture, the other sings beneath it. We were never meant to choose between microscope and psalter; they are the twin lenses of one telescope aimed at the same light.

That light is the thread this book will follow. It is the illumination pain tries to teach, the coherence under chaos, the melody beneath discord. We shall go slowly; truth works best at the pace of breath. First we will face the old paradox—that evil is necessary—and listen until it yields its secret. Then we will watch it dissolve in the realisation that what we called punishment was always instruction. From there we shall trace how love and freedom learn to live together without collapse—a pattern I call the Redemption Optimization. Do not be frightened by the mathematics. They are simply another dialect of awe, a way of speaking with precision what faith has sung for centuries: the universe learns from its errors until only goodness remains. And when the analysis is finished, we shall see that the whole story was never about formulae or philosophy at all; it was about a Father teaching His children how not to hurt one another.

By journey's end, faith will no longer mean believing without evidence, and science will no longer mean observing without wonder. They will stand side by side like two eyes in one face, giving depth to vision. And what they see will be astonishing: a creation not at war with itself but learning, a world resolving its dissonance until only love remains in tune. The search for meaning is not confined to libraries or temples; it walks the streets at dusk when lights bloom behind windows, it sits by the hospital bed where a mother whispers over a fever, it stares from the commuter train's glass, seeing its own face and the city's at once, asking why the day felt both full and hollow. The question is domestic as well as cosmic. It knocks each morning: will today have weight?

Even lips that never shape the word "God" feel the grammar of that question. We want our choices to matter. We want the kindness we offered, the pain we endured, the work we attempted not to vanish like breath upon a mirror. We hunger for permanence within impermanence. No creature longs for food that does not exist; the ache for meaning is itself a sign that meaning is there to be had. When we forget this, the world inclines toward despair. The last century built engines that crossed oceans and engines that erased cities. We found the atom's heart and could not decide whether to worship or weaponise it. Millions perished beneath banners promising salvation by ideology. Progress delivered miracles and nightmares in the same parcel. Philosophers preached absurdity—existence without explanation. Yet even their despair paid a kind of reverence to truth; they still demanded honesty, which is already a moral value. They cursed the silence of heaven, and their anger betrayed their expectation of an answer. A truly indifferent cosmos would not offend us. Only something remembered as loving can break the heart so thoroughly.

Meaning does not die easily. It hides in ruins and builds again. After bombs, poets return to their desks; after plagues, midwives to their doors; after betrayals, lovers dare a second vow. This obstinate return to creation is hope's signature. The universe leans toward repair. Even despair grows weary of itself and begins to pray. To live is to join that repair. Each morning asks whether we will add coherence or confusion. A kind word is a small correction in the moral field; an apology is physics—energy transferred from pride back into relationship. The laws of thermodynamics and the Sermon on the Mount are cousins: both describe the only ways energy can move if life is to last.

The so-called problem of evil is not the only riddle. The deeper puzzle is goodness—why does love keep returning after every disappointment? Why, in spite of millennia of cruelty, do compassion and creativity rise like grass through concrete? Evil explains itself; it is entropy of the heart. Goodness is the true astonishment: it has no natural reason to endure, and yet it does. Every infant's cry is a defiance of nihilism. Walk a forest after fire. The soil is black, apparently sterile; beneath, seeds have waited for this hour. Heat cracks the shell; ash feeds the root. Destruction becomes prelude. So with the soul: conscience germinates in the ashes of regret; pain, listened to, becomes fertilizer for wisdom. This is why mature people carry a certain gentleness; they have burned and sprouted again.

Faith and reason both point to this regenerative logic. The physicist calls it self-organisation; the theologian calls it redemption. The terms differ; the heartbeat is the same. Order re-emerges because love at the foundation refuses to die. Reason, at its best, is reverent—it kneels before consistency and calls it beautiful. Mathematics is worship without confession, a devotion to coherence; every theorem is a psalm in numbers. Faith, at its best, is lucid—it seeks not escape but understanding of why the world still awakens awe. When these two meet, wonder becomes articulate. Reality is not a battlefield between chaos and order but a dialogue eternally resolving toward harmony.

Our ancestors knew as much. The psalmist, staring at the stars, felt terror and tenderness together: "What is man, that Thou art mindful of him?" An astronomer, after seeing the blue earth set against blackness, could have written the same line. Perspective humbles and ennobles at once; our smallness becomes the very reason for our preciousness. We are the universe discovering it can care. In moments of sharp clarity—birth, death, forgiveness—the question of meaning ceases to be theory and becomes air. At a graveside, measurements are absurd; before a newborn, it seems equally absurd that anything so fragile should be entrusted to our shaking hands. Between those astonishments life unfolds, asking reverence. Existence is not an accident to endure or a sentence to serve, but an invitation.

Pain returns here, altered. It is not a flaw but the tutor of empathy. Without suffering, love would remain a pleasant hypothesis; with it, love becomes knowledge. Those who have lost become gentlest; those who have failed, most forgiving. The universe learns mercy by experiencing itself through us. Perhaps this is why silence heals. In quiet, analysis subsides and the hum of coherence can be heard—the same undertone the mystics named oneness and the physicists detect as background radiation. Creation remembers its song. Our age's trouble is not doubt but distraction. We have multiplied signals until the signal itself is lost. To recover meaning is not to add information but to subtract noise; to sit still long enough for gratitude to rise is already to join the repair.

Cynicism will call such hunger naïve. Yet cynicism is disappointment that would not become wisdom. It stands at coherence's gate and refuses to enter for fear of being changed. To seek meaning is the most realistic act of all, for meaning is what reality does: atoms organise, seeds sprout, forgiveness rebuilds. Given time, the universe trends toward understanding. Sanity is to travel with it. Reason's redemption is humility—the wise mind kneels inwardly. Faith's redemption is honesty—the loving heart faces facts. When humility and honesty meet, mystery stops threatening and begins beckoning. The world becomes intelligible, not because we conquer it, but because we consent to it.

By degrees a picture emerges. Pain is instruction, not indictment. Evil is necessary once, never twice. Freedom is the proving-ground of love, not its negation. The universe is not a wound waiting to scab but a pupil mastering the lesson. We are that lesson in flesh. Stand by the sea at night and you can feel it: each wave a question, each returning tide an answer. The dialogue is endless, and the theme is constant—coherence lost, coherence regained. To watch long enough is to pray. Humanity's progress follows the rhythm. Our moral record is feedback written in centuries. We once called conquest glory; now we call it crime. We once forged chains; now we blush at their clink. Not perfectly, not everywhere, yet measurably. The curve of cruelty declines as comprehension rises. The equations of grace are being tested in history, and the graph suggests convergence. Love is learning faster.

If so, hope is not sentiment but observation. Despair misreads the chart—fixating on local storms and ignoring the larger weather. Faith is patience with the trendline; reason supplies the instruments; love interprets the results. All this leads back to one invitation: live as participants, not spectators. Meaning is not a fossil to be found but a light to be kindled by coherence. Each mercy is a theorem proven in motion; each cruelty an error awaiting correction. We are not condemned to repeat the lesson forever. The course is hard, but it ends in graduation. There comes a point in every search when the horizon itself begins to ask questions. We press to the edges of what can be measured and find not blankness but wonder. We can describe atoms and galaxies, but when we ask why there are atoms and galaxies at all, our instruments fall silent. That is not failure; it is invitation.

People ask, "Where did God come from?" and stand, without knowing it, at that very horizon. The question reveals more about us than about Him. We are creatures born within time; we think in sequences—seed and fruit, dawn and dusk—and when asked to imagine what has no beginning, our reason strikes a wall. We can name infinity but not picture it; point toward eternity but not inhabit it. Yet the very attempt betrays something glorious: we notice our limits because we can sense what lies beyond them. Fish do not dream of air; only the creature half-made for sky feels water as constraint. So the power to ask about an uncaused cause is itself a sign that the uncaused exists. If the universe were truly sealed, the question would never arise. We cannot conceive the absolutely impossible, yet we can conceive eternity, perfection, infinity. Appetite implies food; the heart does not hunger for what cannot be. Even "nothing" betrays us. Zero is not nothing; it is a mark within being. True nothingness cannot be imagined; if it cannot be imagined, perhaps it cannot be. If nothing cannot be, then something must always have been. Theology calls that something God—being itself, uncaused, the foundation on which all possibility stands.

Seen thus, "Where did God come from?" is no assault upon faith but a confession of freedom—the mind stretching beyond time. Even scepticism worships here; it warms itself at the same fire from the far side. And what is God in such a frame? Not a distant monarch or a cosmic tinkerer, but the coherence by which all else coheres: love as language, freedom as grammar, humility as music. Creation is not something He once did but something He unceasingly is—the translation of eternity into time. Every atom is a syllable; every conscience, a syntax. Our stories cease to be isolated and become lines within one vast sentence. The moral law is not imposed from without; it resounds from within. We do not so much obey as we harmonise.

Even so, the heart trembles. We are small instruments, easily detuned by grief. A sudden cruelty, a sudden grave—these jar the melody and we cry "why?" into what feels like an indifferent sky. Yet sometimes, after the storm, a faint overtone rises—the sense that our ache participates in a greater heart. Sorrow is love stretching beyond its present form. If pain is the universe learning, if evil is ignorance burning itself out, if love and freedom are meant to dwell together without devouring, then creation is not static but growing—toward coherence as a child grows toward understanding. The laws of physics and the laws of mercy are two languages for one principle: harmony is inevitable once the lesson is loved. Despair imagines a closed system; faith senses an open one. Reason maps the loops; grace gives the energy. Together they reveal that the world is not merely sustained; it is educated. The cosmos is a classroom where wounds become lessons and lessons, at last, become hymns.

There are moments when this is almost visible: a surgeon closing a wound and whispering thanks; a judge choosing mercy over vengeance; a child offering half a broken toy to comfort another. Small acts, yet each alters the moral temperature of the world. Every kindness recalibrates the equation; every forgiveness shortens the distance between earth and heaven. "Why so slow?" we ask. "Why this long schooling of blood and fire?" Because love refuses to coerce. Learning takes time because freedom does. The lesson must be chosen to be real. Coherence cannot be imposed; it must be understood. That patience is what Scripture calls mercy.

And now the horizon shifts from "Whence God?" to "Whither us?" If reality truly learns, its journey must end in stability—what faith calls eternal life. Not mere endless duration, but perfect coherence: love, freedom, and humility balanced forever. Heaven is not the escape from physics but its fulfilment—the world running without error, variables reconciled. In such a state, to understand wholly is to love, and to love wholly is to understand. The scientist and the saint bow over the same mystery, speaking different words for the same light. Every discovery becomes devotion; every prayer becomes an experiment in coherence. From eternity's height, even time's cruelties are transfigured: none erased, all redeemed. The scars of history become the healed tissue of wisdom. As light once came from fire, compassion now comes from pain. The universe wastes no suffering; it recycles sorrow into understanding. When the lesson is finally loved, pain will have nothing left to teach. The equations balance; the music resolves; every discord finds its key. This is not optimism but geometry. Love is the only configuration that survives an infinite test; all else collapses into contradiction.

Thus the search does not end in silence but in symphony. Faith and reason, long estranged, stand together at last like two eyes in one face. They gaze not merely upward to a distant throne but inward to the heart of being, where every law of matter and every law of mercy keep the same time. The fire that once burned now gives light. The lesson is complete, and creation begins its next verse. And if you listen—beneath the engines and the arguments, beneath the pulse of blood and the tick of clocks—you may still hear it: the steady rhythm of coherence beating through all that lives, telling us that all is learning, that nothing is wasted, and that love, after all, is the meaning of meaning itself.

The End of Necessary Evil

THERE IS A STUBBORN pattern in us, woven so deeply into the story of our kind that it feels almost instinctive: we touch the same flame to see if it still burns. Empires have done it, creeds have done it, ideologies have done it. Each comes with its banners and promises—this time, they say, we have learned; this time the world will heal. Yet the script never changes. The proud grow careless, the strong grow cruel, the faithful grow rigid, and what began in light ends again in smoke. We have spent millennia reenacting the first curiosity of Eden—perhaps the rule no longer applies; perhaps we can transgress without consequence—and the scar is always the same, only deeper, etched now not just in flesh but in history's DNA. We inherit the wounds of those who tested the fire before us, and still we test it again, convinced that enlightenment will make us flameproof.

For centuries humanity told itself that suffering was necessary—the tuition of wisdom, the price of progress, the fuel of refinement. We canonized our scars as credentials of insight. "No pain, no gain," we muttered, as though endurance were identical with enlightenment. Even in their noblest hours, religions wrapped pain in sanctity. We built altars to it, baptized it as virtue, and spoke of tragedy as noble, sacrifice as inevitable, grief as the coin by which goodness bought endurance. But what if the old assumption is false? What if pain was never the price of learning at all, but the teacher's note left behind once the lesson was finished—a remnant, not a requirement?

The philosophers meant well when they codified necessity. Augustine[1], striving to absolve God of cruelty, called evil privatio boni—the absence of good, a hole where being faltered. Leibniz[2], anxious to preserve optimism, argued that this was "the best possible world," pain included, because a greater design required contrast. Later thinkers defended freedom by defending harm: if love cannot compel, they reasoned, then God must permit the consequences of choice, however dreadful. The logic is tidy, the conclusion intolerable. Follow it to the end, and you find not comfort but despair—a God who educates by wounding and a universe condemned to retake the same exam forever. If evil must exist eternally, then love has failed its own test. If every generation must bleed for the same revelation, the cosmos is not learning; it is looping.

And yet—what if evil were temporary? What if the fracture of being was a single experiment, necessary once so that creation might never again play out of tune? Then pain becomes not punishment but correction, not condition but completion. The point is not whether pain can teach—it can—but whether it must keep teaching. And if the world itself offers testimony, the answer already glimmers in its fabric. Every living thing knows how to mend. Cut the flesh and cells rush to knit. Scorch a forest and green returns. Break a heart and, in time, it beats again, wiser for the breaking. Creation heals because healing is its grammar. Pain does not sustain it; coherence does. We have mistaken the scar for the lesson. Suffering is not the source of wisdom; it is the echo of unlearned mercy. When understanding dawns, the echo fades.

Reality behaves like a moral intelligence—an organism learning how not to wound its own body. Watch closely and you

1. Augustine, *Confessions*, trans. Henry Chadwick (Oxford: Oxford University Press, 1991), VII.12.

2. G. W. Leibniz, *Theodicy: Essays on the Goodness of God, the Freedom of Man and the Origin of Evil*, trans. E. M. Huggard (London: Routledge & Kegan Paul, 1951), §120.

can see it. When cruelty grows, compassion counterbalances. When lies multiply, truth intensifies its demand. When despair spreads, beauty appears like an antibody. The system corrects; the pattern learns. Creation looks less like a machine grinding toward entropy and more like a consciousness remembering its design. Here theology and science begin to rhyme. The biologist calls it homeostasis, the physicist equilibrium, the mystic grace. All mean the same thing: the universe returns to balance once imbalance is recognized. Pain is not punishment but signal—the feedback of love reminding freedom of its limits. Imagine a cosmos where even cause and effect serve mercy: every action reverberates, teaching the hand that struck how it feels to be struck, until empathy becomes inevitable. Slowly, through a thousand ages, reality educates itself. The lesson is not "do not feel," but "feel rightly"; not "suffer," but "understand."

In that light, the Cross ceases to be a puzzle of suffering and becomes the syllabus of redemption. Love entered its own system and endured rejection not as martyrdom but as demonstration; in that moment pain met comprehension and lost its authority. The world learned what rejection costs; to repeat it is incoherent. And yet humanity continues to test the flame. We call it curiosity, but at its root lies disbelief. We do not yet trust that the lesson holds. So we reenact the same errors, hoping that this time love will bend its law for us. It never does—and it never stops forgiving. Each repetition hurts less because it teaches faster. History's cruelty decays by half-lives, not by decrees.

Still the question remains: if reality learns, what makes it learn well? The answer is not force. We trust coercion more easily than freedom because coercion feels efficient. We imagine virtue as discipline imposed, order as obedience enforced. But the Master Teacher works otherwise. Love persuades by light, not pressure. Truth convinces by clarity, not fear. Seen clearly, rebellion looks absurd; understood fully, evil becomes impossible to repeat. Heaven, therefore, is not a reward for rule-keepers but a society of the comprehending. It is not a gated city for the obedient, but an open world of the awakened—beings who have discovered that the opposite of law is not freedom but incoherence. The child who burns her hand once learns not by decree but by memory. The difference between hell and heaven is whether one insists on touching the flame again.

Every act of rejection opens harm; every act of forgiveness closes it. Because the universe keeps moral accounts, wounds can only diminish as understanding spreads. Evil was necessary once, but not twice. Once love learned how to endure rejection without ceasing to love, the curriculum was complete. The Cross is that moment—the mathematical zero where harm cancels itself out. A theologian calls it grace; a physicist might call it the global minimum of pain. Beyond that point, only ignorance can suffer needlessly. If the law is real, its traces should appear across life, and they do. When evil's supposed necessity ends, struggle does not vanish—ignorance does. Growth continues, but the lash retires. Discipline remains and becomes friendship with truth. Science still questions, art still dreams, faith still worships. Only cruelty is outdated. Each generation inherits fewer respectable excuses for harm; slavery, persecution, exploitation—once uttered with pride—now sound like relics from a primitive tongue. The moral gradient of history tilts toward coherence. The world is remembering its lesson. When the lesson is loved, the lash is needless.

If the universe truly learns, its lessons should be traceable not only in the private miracles of conscience but in the slow evolution of culture itself. History begins to look less like a chain of accidents and more like the world's own autobiography—a diary of awakening written in consequences. Each epoch records an experiment, a failure, a correction. Progress is not a straight ascent but a series of forgiven errors. One can almost hear creation thinking. At first the pattern is violent, the learning crude. Tribes discover that vengeance, while satisfying for a moment, multiplies instability. Empires rise on the thrill of conquest only to collapse beneath the weight of fear. Religions attempt to codify virtue by decree, but law without love petrifies into judgment. The same cycle repeats—rebellion, punishment, reform, relapse—the moral equivalent of tectonic plates grinding until they learn to rest. For millennia the world has rehearsed the same lesson: power without compassion collapses inward; freedom without humility devours itself.

Yet beneath the surface the feedback works. The intervals between collapses lengthen; the scale of cruelty shrinks. Where once the strong enslaved without conscience, now conscience enslaves the strong. We still harm, but we hesitate; the hesitation is proof that the universe remembers. If there is a divine pedagogy, this is it: creation permitted to feel the cost of its own misuse until comprehension becomes irreversible. Evil's existence, then, is not a flaw in design but an allowance for learning—necessary once to show freedom its edges, never again. Once the creature knows what suffering means, to cause it intentionally is not ignorance but madness.

Scripture tells this in its own poetry. The law is given, broken, reinterpreted; prophets rage; people repent; the cycle repeats until the Word Himself enters the equation. The Incarnation is the moment the Author steps into His own text, not to erase it but to demonstrate how it reads when spoken perfectly. Christ's life is divine syntax compiled without error. His death is the system crash that exposes what corrupted the code. His resurrection is the reboot—the living proof that love survives every exception the universe can throw. And the Cross, that old scandal, is not punishment so much as pedagogy, the highest demonstration of feedback ever enacted: the world poured out its rejection; love absorbed it without returning harm; the loop closed. The signal of mercy propagated through the moral field of existence, and nothing has cancelled it since. What theologians call grace; a mathematician could call convergence.

In the centuries following, that convergence became visible. Slavery, once considered infrastructure, began to look monstrous. Torture, once sport, became crime. War, once glory, began to feel obscene. The distance between those transformations is measurable. Humanity is learning, and its moral data show an unmistakable trend: the half-life of cruelty is shrinking. Pain decays when understanding rises. Yet understanding is slow, and love will not violate the tempo of consent. Coherence cannot be forced; it must be chosen. And so the great Teacher waits, patient as gravity, while we test and retest what has already been proved. His patience offends us; we demand intervention. Why does injustice still breathe? Why does pain still echo? Perhaps the answer is embedded in the question. The universe is not neglected; it is trusted—to finish the lesson freely. The moment virtue is compelled, its substance dissolves. The moral law is like a violin: too tight a string snaps; too loose a string sags; but when love and freedom are tuned in perfect tension, the world begins to sing.

This is why coercion cannot sustain paradise. Heaven, as Christ described it, is not a fortress of obedience but a fellowship of comprehension. Its citizens are not controlled; they are coherent. They have understood at last that every act of harm is self-harm, every cruelty a wound to the one who inflicts it. The soul that truly sees this cannot sin again—not for lack of ability, but for lack of appetite. Evil becomes not forbidden but boring. We glimpse this even now in the way understanding alters desire: the addict who truly comprehends the cost of compulsion ceases to crave it; the tyrant awakened to empathy cannot continue his tyranny without nausea. Once the mind has seen the pattern, ignorance is no longer possible. The serpent of repetition loses its teeth.

Here lies the genius of divine pedagogy: love wastes no pain. Every sorrow, every failure, every betrayal becomes data for the great optimization. Repentance is not humiliation but recalibration—the soul rewriting its own code in light of new understanding. Forgiveness is the merging of corrected files. Even guilt, that tormenting reminder of what we have done, is grace in larval form—the system pinging us to apply the update. And history, that chaotic archive, is the record of each update applied. The abolition of slavery was not merely political; it was metaphysical. It signified a rise in the universe's comprehension constant, λ—the rate at which love learns. Each reform, each act of mercy, increases λ; each cruelty slows it but cannot reverse it. Once λ is greater than zero, evil is mathematically doomed. Despair, though understandable, is illogical: to believe goodness will fail is to deny the structure of existence. Reality's direction is fixed. Love is not a mood but the equilibrium of being. Entropy wins in closed systems; love opens them.

If we could see history as God sees it, we would measure progress not in empires but in empathy, not in power but in perception. The prophets did not predict technology; they foresaw tenderness. "The meek shall inherit the earth" is not sentiment; it describes the final configuration of consciousness. Once humility proves more adaptive than pride, evolution completes its arc. Science, for all its different language, keeps discovering the same trajectory: cooperation outcompetes aggression in ecosystems; reciprocal trust yields higher survival than domination; repeated games favor honesty over betrayal. The universe rewards coherence. The laws of physics seem quietly biased toward love.

In the human heart the same algorithm runs. Every time we forgive, we close a feedback loop. Every apology restores energy to the moral circuit. Every act of empathy reduces the system's potential for chaos. These are not metaphors but mechanics: forgiveness is moral thermodynamics; the universe learns through us. And because learning cannot be rushed, the Teacher waits. Patience is not indifference but confidence in the outcome. The Cross—that single moment when perfect love met perfect rejection—is proof that the equation converges. Pain's function was fulfilled; the derivative of suffering became zero. Everything since has been application, not experiment.

It is abstract only until it is personal. Each of us is a microcosm of this computation. Within our lives the same variables interact—love, freedom, humility striving toward balance. Each choice alters the local field of coherence. When we lash out in pride, the equation trembles; when we repent, it restabilizes. The laws of moral physics operate as faithfully in the kitchen as in the cosmos. To live kindly is not to deny the world's pain but to cooperate with its healing. Each act of mercy is a small verification of the universal theorem; the more such verifications occur, the faster the convergence. Grace is not a miracle imposed from outside but a process emerging from within—a resonance between divine intention and human participation.

At times the resonance sounds faint. Headlines of cruelty drown it. But listen across centuries and the melody is unmistakable: violence, though louder, is shorter-lived; compassion, though quiet, sustains. The world hums in the key of restoration. The question is not whether pain can teach—it can—but whether love has finally learned. Every sign suggests that it has. We still burn our fingers on the old flame, but the interval between touch and recoil shortens; understanding accelerates. One day, the memory of burning will suffice; no one will need to test the fire again. The saints called this sanctification; the scientist might call it convergence to equilibrium. Both name the same thing: the stabilization of being around love.

That is why Christ's final word was not defeat but notation: Finished. Not "I am finished," but It is.[3] The function has reached its asymptote; the loop has closed. What remains is application—integration—the slow spread of understanding through every node of creation. The Cross was never about appeasing wrath; it was about demonstrating coherence. It shows what happens when perfect love encounters perfect freedom without rejection: the equation resolves. Pain, as pedagogy, is complete; any further suffering is remedial work in hearts that have not yet caught up to what reality already knows. In that sense every cruelty today is not a new evil but an old lesson repeating in a corner of the classroom where the light has not yet reached. The curriculum is over; some have not finished reading the notes.

So, the task remains: carry understanding into unlit rooms—teach not by conquest but by contagion of mercy. The gospel, stripped of ornament, is this: the universe has learned not to wound, and we are invited into its comprehension. When the lesson is finished, what remains is not silence but understanding. The fire burns only until it has nothing left to teach; after that its work is memory. What we have called "the problem of evil" was never a riddle to be solved but a course to be completed. Creation has been learning—slowly and at immense cost—what love requires to stay coherent. Once that lesson is secure, pain retires with dignity.

3. John 19:30. The Greek *tetelestai* carries the sense of completion or fulfillment.

A world that has learned would not be a world without movement. There would still be growth and inquiry and the unfolding of wonder, but no longer growth by breaking. Life's rhythm would continue, only now in tune. Discipline would not vanish; it would take the form of joy—the steady pleasure of alignment. What was once called obedience would be recognized as understanding. Heaven is not a place where nothing happens, but where everything happens in harmony. We struggle to imagine such existence because our peace has always followed struggle; we assume drama must be written in the key of danger. But if danger truly ended—if love had learned to live with freedom—the story would not stop; it would deepen. The characters would no longer wrestle for survival; they would create for joy. The stage would remain, the light still fall upon it, but the play would change its tone. It would become, at last, a comedy in the old holy sense: a story that ends in restoration.

Pain, then, is not the author of wisdom, only its reluctant tutor. It taught what it had to teach, and now the world remembers. We see hints of that remembering everywhere. Cruelty, once justified as strength, has become shame. Domination, once called destiny, now sounds primitive. Every century adds prohibitions against harm, as though humanity were recovering its native language. We are beginning to understand that suffering was never divine necessity, only divine concession—the temporary scaffolding of learning. When the structure stands, the scaffolding falls. If love and freedom are to last forever, they must become one movement; freedom that harms is not yet free, and love that coerces is not yet love. Their reconciliation was the great experiment of creation and reached its proof at the Cross. There love absorbed every rejection and remained itself; from that point forward, pain could continue only as echo, not instruction. It lingers where comprehension has not yet dawned, but the curriculum itself is complete.

"Go, and sin no more,"[4] said Christ—not as threat but as announcement. The test was over; understanding had arrived. Sin remains only where comprehension has not yet reached, like

4. John 8:11.

darkness in valleys after the sun has risen. Our task is to carry that light into those shadows—not to explain pain, but to end it. And the work of ending it will not be violence against the world but patient restoration. Each forgiveness, each moment of courage, each refusal to repeat a harm is part of that repair. History is the classroom where this closure unfolds; what we call progress is simply the growing accuracy of love.

Beyond the classroom lies the world after fire. It is not a new creation replacing the old, but the old awakened. The mountains will still stand, the seas still breathe, but their language will have changed. Time will no longer rush; it will flow. Knowledge will not divide; it will clarify. The arts will not protest but praise. The sciences will not explain away wonder but increase it. The kingdoms of this world will not vanish; they will be transfigured into service. For the first time since the beginning, everything will make sense. We call that state paradise—not the end of learning, but the end of misunderstanding. The mind will still explore, yet not to repair what was broken but to rejoice in what is true. The heart will still feel, but without fear of loss. The body will still move, but never against the soul. Love will have learned to last, and so it will rest.

Seen from this height, evil reveals itself as ignorance pretending to be wisdom—a student copying the same wrong answer until the Teacher, in mercy, writes Finished on the board. From that moment the repetition ends. We will still walk and still discover, but we shall walk toward light, not away from it. Every question will lead to another answer, and every answer will deepen delight; knowledge and joy will no longer compete. And when at last every path of harm is closed, we shall see that redemption was never a rescue from life—it was life, finally coherent, existence reunited with its own meaning. The story will not end; it will simply stop bleeding. The flame that once burned will still give light, but no more pain. Love will remain, not as sentiment but as law—the equilibrium of being itself. Then the universe, having learned the lesson of love, will be at peace with itself at last.

Part II: The Redemption Optimization

The Key Equation

Part 1: The Awakening of Law

EVERY LONG SEARCH REACHES a moment when language tires of its own eloquence. Metaphor circles the truth so many times it grows dizzy; the mind, starved of gravity, longs for a law that will hold it still. I reached that point one sleepless night while the house lay silent and my desk lay buried beneath papers—half-legible diagrams, stray quotations, arrows leaping from margin to margin. I had been tracing how harm travels through the world: how one wound begets another, how forgiveness interrupts the chain, how love seems to repair faster than hatred can destroy. Each time the pattern began to appear, it dissolved again like mist under light. Then, almost shyly, symmetry stepped forward. Every genuine act of love reduced disorder faster than retaliation could increase it. The numbers whispered what poets had been saying all along. Philosophy began to behave like physics.

I remember the question rising almost against my will: *Could redemption itself obey an equation?* Not to trap mercy in symbols, but to test its coherence. For if grace is real, it must also be reliable; and if divine love governs reality, its constancy should bear the steadiness of law. It was a terrifying thought, because it implied that faith might be measurable—and therefore falsifiable. But truth that cannot be tested is not yet truth; it is only admiration. Love deserves the honour of verification.

The machinery of creation is obsessed with balance. Heat spreads, motion slows, energy levels seek rest. Entropy—the long accounting of matter—collects every unpaid debt until equilibrium is restored. And yet the moral life seems to climb against that slope. Kindness runs uphill; courage refuses gravity; forgiveness reverses decay. We spend moral energy to raise good out of ruin. On the surface this looks like defiance of the second law of thermodynamics, but perhaps it is not rebellion at all. Perhaps it is completion. Maybe what we call goodness is not a violation of physics but its next iteration—entropy running backward through consciousness, meaning reclaiming the energy that chaos abandoned. The universe may not be bleeding meaning; it may be learning coherence.

That, in essence, is the claim I have come to call *The Redemption Optimization*. It imagines reality as a living algorithm whose purpose is closure—the completion of every unfinished act of love. Physics conserves energy; redemption conserves mercy. Every time good is chosen freely, the fabric of being tightens a little, as if the world were remembering itself. Freedom remains, but folly loses glamour. Evil becomes statistically uninteresting. Good does not triumph by noise; it triumphs by making harm improbable.

Such an idea would have sounded mystical if the evidence had not insisted on behaving like law. Wherever I looked, the pattern repeated: in ecosystems healing after fire, in families reconciling after betrayal, in nations repenting after war. Restoration followed injury not by chance but by rhythm—as if reality were built with feedback loops that refuse despair. The further I followed that rhythm, the more it resembled the equations of growth and decay that describe every self-correcting system.

All survival, I began to see, is feedback. Touch flame—learn. Lie—feel shame—tell truth—learn again. Conscience is feedback, the echo of coherence in the human heart. Civilizations obey the same law: trial, error, repentance, repair. Creation itself seems structured for reconciliation. In mathematical shorthand one might write:

$$dC/dt = R(C) - E(t)$$

where C stands for coherence, $R(C)$ for restoration, $E(t)$ for injury through time. If restoration outruns harm, coherence rises; if harm outruns restoration, the system decays. The symbols matter less than the music they describe: correction faster than corruption, mercy stronger than entropy.

When seen this way, redemption ceases to be miracle and becomes metabolism—the moral physics of a universe that refuses to stay wounded.

History itself, viewed over millennia, bears the same pattern written in the slow ink of centuries. We can plot its moral data as a physicist plots temperature. Violence per capita declines; empathy expands; cruelty loses its sanction. Conquest once counted as glory; now it is disgrace. Slavery once underwrote economies; now it is condemned by conscience. The distance between those pairs of sentences is measurable coherence—redemption's constant, rising through time. Something in the moral field of humanity is remembering its first equation. Each generation inherits the residue of harm and the instruments of faster repair. That acceleration is grace quantified.

Yet even grace has boundaries, and the boundary of redemption is freedom. Love cannot compel its own triumph, for compulsion cancels the experiment. The Maker designed a universe that must persuade, never enslave. Picture a violin string: freedom is its length, love the tension. Too tight, and the string snaps—tyranny. Too loose, and the tone collapses—anarchy. Only when length and tension consent together does music appear. That is why God seems patient. Coherence cannot be hurried without becoming coercion; grace moves at the speed of consent.

The more I examined that law, the more it explained the very texture of divine history. Revelation unfolds as an education paced to human willingness. Every commandment, every covenant, every incarnation respects freedom's tempo. God does not shout; He waits for the ear to be ready. The patience that once looked like absence is revealed as precision—the refusal to force what can only be understood.

And so The Redemption Optimization is not a sterile equation written across the sky but a living grammar written into the pulse of existence. It tells us that the universe is not neutral. It leans toward healing. Evil may roar for a time, but its mathematics are already against it.

Part 2—The Working Equation

Every law that claims truth must eventually touch the ground. Beauty in theory is not enough; reality demands evidence. If grace is truly a force, then we should find its traces not only in scripture and conscience but in the behaviour of the world itself.

I began, therefore, to ask how harm actually declines. In the moral field, as in physics, decay follows pattern. What is wounded seeks repair; what is forgiven ceases to multiply. If we could write this process in the language of time, it would read something like:

$$E(t) = E_1 \cdot e^{-\lambda t}$$

Here $E(t)$ names the amount of active harm, E_1 the first injury—the primordial refusal when creation first discovered rejection—and λ (lambda) the rate at which love learns. If λ is greater than zero, evil decays: slowly at first, then with accelerating mercy. Spiritually translated, forgiveness begins to outpace guilt. Once the lesson is loved, pain forgets how to teach.

This is the moral half-life of evil. It does not vanish by decree but by comprehension. Each act of understanding lowers the residue of suffering. The world learns what not to repeat. The ancient theologians intuited this when they said that sin was "folly" and repentance "illumination." They were describing, without equations, a system that corrects its own error.

The same rhythm appears in history. Consider the great arc of cruelty: slavery, once common as soil, now outlawed; torture, once entertainment, now horror; conquest, once virtue, now crime. The moral temperature rises—slowly, unevenly, but irreversibly. The graphs of violence plotted across centuries slope downward; the graphs of empathy and human rights climb. The pattern is statistical grace. Humanity's λ is increasing.

These are not accidents of culture. They are the fingerprints of convergence—the world remembering the logic written into its foundation. Every generation inherits the debris of old evil and the tools for quicker restoration. That acceleration is what the prophets called the coming of the kingdom, what the scientist might call moral evolution, and what the mathematician names positive feedback toward coherence.

Yet every optimization has its constraint, and here the constraint is sacred. Redemption must operate within freedom or it ceases to be redemption. Love can persuade, never coerce. The Maker did not design a universe of marionettes but of partners. Each consent enlarges the field; each refusal delays it. Hence the strange patience of history. God seems slow because He refuses to force the result.

Picture again the violin string: freedom defines the length, love the tension, humility the hand that tunes. Too tight, and the string breaks—tyranny. Too slack, and the note dies—chaos. Only in balance does sound become song. That, perhaps, is the secret architecture of providence: harmony achieved through voluntary resonance. The law cannot be rushed; it unfolds at the speed of understanding.

When viewed through this lens, the Cross ceases to be mere tragedy and becomes the pivot of the moral universe. Extend the curve of harm backward through time and there is a moment where it touches zero—the instant when love absorbed every rejection and still remained love. That is the fixed point of the system, the asymptote where the function of suffering reaches its limit and cannot rise again. From that point forward the equation continues, approaching perfection without compulsion, forever free.

Perhaps that is why Christ's final word was *Finished.* It was not resignation but notation—the moral books balanced, the variable of vengeance solved. The fabric of reality had reached stability.

Evil could still echo, but it could no longer instruct. The data of history since then are the slow confirmation of that theorem.

From this vantage, redemption is not anomaly but algorithm: a continuous integration process where every act of love merges into the new build of being. Grace is the background process of existence—quiet, persistent, reconciling. Each prayer is a handshake protocol; each mercy a successful merge. Repentance is simply accepting the update.

Humanity is therefore not a spectator of salvation but its collaborator. The program still runs. Every kindness is another data point confirming the model; every cruelty, a lingering outlier awaiting correction. We are the agents debugging creation from within. Each honest choice raises λ; each reconciliation closes another file in the world's moral archive.

This vision turns familiar virtues into acts of physics. To forgive is to accelerate decay; to tell the truth is to restore lost information; to love without demand is to stabilize the field. Even a wise silence—when it prevents harm—adds measurable coherence to the system. The saints were not escapists defying matter; they were physicists of the soul, experimenting with the constants of grace.

The proof of this law is not confined to saints. Every level of creation shows the same bias toward healing. Forests regenerate after fire, bodies scar instead of dissolving, societies rebuild after catastrophe. The pattern is not perfection yet, but convergence. Evil's half-life shortens as comprehension spreads. The universe is tutoring itself, and we are its willing students.

Part 3—The Symphony of Completion

Every great system, once understood, reveals not only order but beauty. So it is with the law of redemption. What began as a question of coherence becomes, in the end, a song of gratitude. The more we understand how grace works, the more awe it awakens. Law, rightly seen, is not the enemy of wonder but its grammar—the clarity that allows astonishment to speak without dissolving into chaos. To say that redemption is optimized is not to mechanize mercy but to marvel that mercy is consistent. The universe is not arbitrary in its kindness; it is faithful. Understanding does not cool devotion; it refines it. Knowledge, when married to reverence, becomes worship in its highest form.

This, I think, is what Lewis[1] meant when he said that to understand something rightly is to love it more, not less. When we glimpse the mechanics of forgiveness, we do not diminish its mystery; we behold its precision. Every symbol in our equation becomes an act of praise—lambda as the patience of God, E(t) as the fading memory of sin, C(t) as coherence expanding toward infinity. Mathematics bows to theology; theology smiles through mathematics. The world reveals its Maker not by exception but by reliability.

For in this cosmos, evil is not equal and opposite to good. It is an event already decaying. Every injustice carries the seed of its own correction; every scar stores information for future wisdom. Even entropy, that stern accountant of physics, becomes servant to grace. It ensures that nothing harmful endures untransformed. Pain is converted to knowledge; loss becomes empathy; time itself acts as the great solvent of cruelty. In that light, redemption is not magic but mathematics made merciful—the science of learning not to wound.

When love leads and freedom follows, the system stabilizes. When fear leads and coercion follows, the system oscillates until exhaustion. The gospel, translated into technical language, is simply the universe discovering the stable configuration of love. All else—war, greed, tyranny, despair—are transient instabilities, noise that will one day smooth into harmony.

Our role, then, is not to admire the theorem from afar but to live inside its proof. We stand as agents within the great optimization, each life a laboratory where love is tested and confirmed. Every generation inherits unfinished equations—old hatreds, new technologies, unresolved fears—and is invited to reduce the error term. The instruments are ancient and plain: repentance,

1. C. S. Lewis, *Mere Christianity* (New York: HarperOne, 2001), bk. 4, chap. 9.

forgiveness, compassion, creativity, truth. Each is a calibration, a correction in the cosmic algorithm.

To pray is to align our variables with coherence. To love an enemy is to raise λ in the local field. To tell the costly truth is to feed energy back into the moral circuit. Even silence, when it restrains harm, contributes to the sum of healing. The smallest act done in love alters the trajectory of the universe, however slightly. Nothing coherent is ever lost; every mercy leaves its mark.

Hope, then, is not wishful thinking but confidence in a measurable trend. Once the line of coherence begins to rise, it cannot fall without contradiction. The universe has seen what love can do; it cannot unlearn it. Despair misreads the graph by staring at local turbulence and ignoring global convergence. Faith is the willingness to trust the long dataset of God's memory. The mean of mercy increases; the variance of evil declines. Over infinite time, the function approaches perfection.

And so the story of redemption ends not in silence but in symphony. Salvation can be sung as hymn and written as theorem—the same melody replayed until even the most discordant instrument learns its part. Where love leads and freedom consents, the music resolves; where rejection lingers, the melody pauses, patient for the wandering note. Evil instructs once; good remembers forever. The final proof is not a formula but a harmony—the sound of creation reaching its cadence.

Imagine that last movement: the choir of galaxies resonating in phase, every will free, every heart tuned. The moral equation at last complete:

$$E(t) \to 0, \quad C(t) \to \infty$$

Harm extinct. Coherence everlasting. Love without bound. This is the law beneath the gospel and the gospel within the law: the universe is learning not to wound.

When that learning is complete, what we now call heaven will simply be clarity—the full comprehension of what mercy has been doing all along. Time will no longer measure decay but deepen joy.

Every creature, every consciousness, will know its own equation within the larger proof: "I was forgiven; therefore, I exist." Existence itself will have become thanksgiving.

And perhaps, when the last dissonance dissolves, when every scar has turned to story and every story to song, we will hear the laughter of the One who wrote the code and entered it Himself. The mathematician will close His notebook, not because there are no more problems, but because every problem has become praise.

Then love, freedom, and coherence will be one; mercy will be the atmosphere we breathe; and reality, at last, will know what it has been trying to say since the beginning:

Finished—and alive forever.

The Moral Kernel Optimization

The Law of Bounded Harm

Part 1—The Discovery of Boundaries

EVERY CRAFTSMAN KNOWS THAT beauty endures only within its bounds. A violin must keep its pitch or the music goes ragged; a bridge must carry weight within its tolerances or grace becomes rubble; even a flame must learn its reach, for beyond a certain point it ceases to give light and begins to devour. Boilers have gauges; gardens have fences; the galaxies themselves keep to their paths by an invisible reticence we have learned to call law. Endurance is never an accident. It is freedom held in form—liberty taught its own dimensions. And yet, when we come to moral life, we grow strangely forgetful. We applaud "infinite love," "unbounded generosity," "limitless compassion"—excellent phrases, all of them, until they drift from proportion and become the slogans by which zeal excuses its trespasses. We vow to do "whatever it takes" for a righteous end, meaning well, until our goodness begins to spend other people's pain. Whenever passion outruns reverence for limits, tragedy follows as the shadow follows the body. Every tyranny begins with the same confident announcement: *It is necessary.*

The Moral Kernel Optimization was framed to forbid that bargain. It says, very simply, that if love and freedom are to last forever, they must travel within guardrails that refuse harm as currency. Without those rails, compassion becomes manipulation and virtue reduces to arithmetic. The kernel is not a new conscience but a clear translation of the old one: no good end may be purchased by deliberate cruelty, however handsomely the ledger smiles. For a long time we were seduced by tidier sums—*maximize happiness, minimize pain*—as though the universe were an accountant balancing pleasures against griefs. But such formulae, once laid upon flesh-and-blood, tear at the seams. Someone always ends by paying the bill who did not agree to the purchase. History's ledgers are crowded with these transactions: a slave ship launched "for commerce," a guillotine raised "for equality," a laboratory made cruel "for knowledge," a bomb dropped "to end all wars." Each was defended by its arithmetic—sacrifice the few for the many; spend pain now to save it later—and yet the numbers never add, because the coin is counterfeit. Human suffering is not fungible. It cannot be averaged, exchanged, or offset. To harm one person intentionally "for the sake of others" is not moral algebra but amnesia; it forgets what a person is.

The moment harm is chosen as an instrument, goodness collapses—not poetically but mathematically. The act has left what the mathematicians would call the feasible domain: that region of choice within which love and freedom can coexist. Beyond that boundary every calculation becomes undefined. You may no longer compare outcomes, because the first premise—the irreducible dignity of the subject—has been thrown away. Evil cannot be optimized. A calculus that spends people is not mathematics at all; it is forgetting made into policy. Picture a narrow road along a mountain's edge. Guardrails do not insult the driver; they preserve the journey. To tear them out in the name of liberty is merely to invite the mountain's swift reply. So it is in moral space. Boundaries are not barriers to freedom; they are what make freedom navigable. They tell us where motion remains flight and where it thins into a fall. In every science a problem must declare its constraints before it can be solved; in moral life the constraints are the conditions under which love and freedom remain coherent. Outside them the system crashes—cruelty disguised as principle, necessity impersonating virtue. Trace any moral catastrophe to its spring, and you will find the same breach: harm pressed into service as a tool.

The kernel therefore asks one question, always the same and deceptively plain: Does this choice increase intentional harm, or does it heal it? If harm rises by design, the action is out of bounds. No arithmetic can make it wise. If our reasoning is to remain stable, we must refuse to treat destruction as a variable to be "managed," and receive it instead as a signal to stop. This is not innovation; it is the oldest wisdom dressed in modern clothes. The prophets said, "I desire mercy, not sacrifice."[1] The Stoics urged life in accordance with nature. Kant[2] insisted that humanity be treated always as an end, never merely as a means. All three were describing one geometry: coherence holds only when love and freedom are bounded by non-violence. Once harm is willed as a means, the structure buckles; you cannot optimize what has departed the domain of sense. Yet every age has tried. Empires, ideologies, even churches have attempted to redeem cruelty by purpose. They built pyres for purity, prisons for peace, weapons for justice—each persuading itself that it was the necessary exception—and each discovering, in time, that the rule does not negotiate. The moral field has its own conservation law: harm, once chosen, cannot produce coherence. The price of crossing the boundary is always collapse.

It is no accident, then, that Christ's great law is phrased not as expansion but as restraint: Love your neighbour as yourself.[3] Not more than, not instead of, but as. There is a divine symmetry in that word which keeps compassion from condescension and freedom from appetite. It is the guardrail of proportion. And so the kernel's first insight is humility. Moral genius lies less in inventing new rules than in remembering the limits that make goodness possible. The most dangerous words in any tongue are "for the greater good," when they mean "for my preferred good." Once we make suffering into currency, we have already spent love. For

1. Hosea 6:6; cf. Matthew 9:13.

2. Immanuel Kant, *Groundwork of the Metaphysics of Morals*, trans. Mary Gregor (Cambridge: Cambridge University Press, 1998), 4:429.

3. Matthew 22:39; Mark 12:31.

that reason, the kernel begins with a stark axiom: no suffering-as-currency. Pain may instruct, but it may never be traded. Any system that buys with harm purchases its own decay. Goodness cannot borrow cruelty and remain coherent.

Part 2—The Chemistry of Healing

Harm never simply vanishes. It lingers, waiting—not for amnesia, but for transfiguration. Time alone cannot erase it, nor decree, nor denial. The wound must be taught what to become. This is the quiet alchemy of grace: the turning of pain into understanding. When flesh mends, it does not erase the cut; it closes it. The skin remembers without reopening. So it is with the conscience and with communities. Forgiveness is the mending of the spirit—the slow drawing together of what was torn until life can circulate again. Every resentment left unhealed is a live wire, sparking in the dark. To forgive is not to forget; it is to make whole.

If the universe indeed runs on feedback—as every living thing does—then forgiveness is the highest feedback: correction without destruction. It is the moral immune system of creation, the ancient instinct by which life resists decay. When mercy flows, infection stops; when it is withheld, the disease spreads—from heart to heart, house to house, nation to nation. The chemistry of grievance is as real as any in the body. A spirit sickened with vengeance poisons its own blood. Empathy, then, is not softness but health—the body's defence against moral entropy. It binds what has been scattered so that coherence may return. Resentment, by contrast, corrodes; it traps the soul in endless rehearsal of the wound, mistaking pain for identity. The only cure is release.

Forgiveness, true forgiveness, is not the indulgence of forgetting, but the courage of remembrance made harmless. It looks evil full in the face, names it, refuses to bless it, yet refuses also to chain the future to it. Mercy remembers in order to restore. That is why the Cross stands at the centre of moral history—not because it denied evil, but because it met it and would not echo it. In that refusal, eternity learned repair. We may describe the same mystery in the language of learning. Each act of comprehension turns harm into instruction; each act of forgiveness turns instruction into wisdom. Where harm once circulated, meaning now flows. Forgiveness is not sentiment but transformation—the rewriting of the moral data until the system is stable again. Theologians called this redemption; a physicist might call it the closure of a loop. Let us give it a symbol—Φ, the moral constant of transfiguration: the point at which pain ceases to accuse and begins to teach. Every act of mercy raises Φ; the higher it climbs, the faster harm decays. Societies rich in Φ grow tender; those impoverished of it grow brittle. Empires do not crumble when their weapons fail but when their mercy runs dry.

Yet grace works only in truth. To forgive falsely is to varnish rot. A physician does not heal by pretending the wound was never there; she cleanses it, though it sting. Grace, too, must name what it redeems. Only when wrong is fully known can forgiveness finish its chemistry; a lie seals the infection in. But when the work is honest, the miracle multiplies. Every release sends a quiet wave outward. One reconciled friendship steadies a household; one mended household steadies a community. Goodness, like contagion, spreads by contact. The mathematics of mercy are exponential.

Some fear that boundaries shrink love—that forbidding vengeance or sacrifice makes life too narrow for passion. But the opposite is true. Without limits, love burns through its own fuel and dies; within them, it learns to shine steady. The moral guardrails are not prison walls but the ribs of a living body—they give shape so the heart can beat freely within. Imagine a society where harm is never treated as currency, where every wound must close where it opened, where pain is not a tool but a tutor. Such a people would cease to glorify suffering. They would remember it only as education complete. Art would turn from despair to wonder. Justice would cease to avenge and begin to repair. Freedom would deepen, because no one would need armour against unseen debts of cruelty.

This is no fantasy. It is the direction of all moral history. Each time humanity draws a new boundary—abolishing slavery, forbidding torture, outlawing coercion—it is not growing fragile but coherent. Every new limit is a discovery: *Here is a line love must not cross if it is to remain love.* And once learned, such lines are not easily forgotten. Even when we fail them, memory tugs us back. The moral field itself has a kind of memory, its gradient tilts toward coherence. We underestimate the speed of grace. We count the wars but not the treaties, the betrayals but not the daily mercies. Yet the long record reveals a steady incline: violence declining, dignity spreading, empathy becoming the instinct rather than the exception. The lesson is being learned. Creation is remembering its own heart.

Physics teaches that entropy never reverses without input; in the moral world, love is that input. Where love enters, decay loses its grip. Harm may not vanish, but its half-life shortens. Forgiveness is the world's slow restoration to coherence. And though history's graphs waver and flare, the line of best fit is clear: cruelty waning, compassion gaining speed. The chemistry of healing can be written as three axioms, simple to speak and endless to apply:

No harm as currency—no good can be bought with pain.

Harm decays by closure—every act of understanding or forgiveness seals a breach in the moral field.

Grace multiplies when shared—every reconciliation strengthens the whole.

Within these bounds, life may learn forever without destroying itself. This is the true optimization of the moral world—not control, but restoration. And when such laws are obeyed long enough, fear itself begins to retire. The human heart, once braced for every blow, begins at last to breathe unguarded. Communities find courage again; freedom becomes safe. That is the secret purpose of every true guardrail—not to restrain life, but to make joy sustainable. Forgiveness is not the end of justice but its perfection. Justice seeks balance; forgiveness achieves it. In that balance the universe itself finds rest—not the stillness of exhaustion, but of harmony, when every note has found its pitch and every wound its healing.

Part 3—The Civilization of Mercy

The world, though weary, is not wandering. It is learning. Each century writes, in the trembling hand of experience, what goodness requires—though the ink is often blood. Every statute born of compassion, every boundary that forbids cruelty, every conscience awakened is another correction in the vast manuscript of creation. We are, each of us, editors in a text begun before time, mending the lines pride first mis-spelled. The Moral Kernel—the law of bounded harm—is simply the grammar by which this editing may continue without tearing the page.

A society's first duty is remembrance. Forgetfulness is the root of relapse; memory, the seed of mercy. The civilizations that endured were not those with the sharpest swords but those that remembered their wounds. Rome fell when it forgot its Republic; Christendom sickened when it forgot Christ; the modern world trembles when it forgets humility. The nations that will last are those that keep the record of compassion sacred. Their monuments will not be statues of conquest but hospitals, libraries, and reconciled families.

Boundaries, far from chaining progress, are what make progress intelligible. Remove the guardrails and even virtue drives off the cliff. Zeal without restraint becomes fanaticism; freedom without patience, chaos. The civilized heart is one that has accepted the limits of love—the knowledge that to harm deliberately, even for noble ends, is to sabotage the very good one seeks to defend. No revolution founded in hatred has ever reaped a harvest worth its price.

If humanity has one collective vocation, it is to become trustworthy with power. For ages we have mistaken strength for license—the license to rule, to exploit, to dominate. But power without humility is fire without air: it burns until nothing remains to burn. Only when power consents to serve does it become creative. That is the kernel's final lesson—coercion cannot build coherence. Empires raised on fear may roar for a season, but their echoes fade into dust. Gentleness builds the structures that outlive marble.

The future belongs to those who learn to govern without violence, to persuade without deceit, to correct without humiliation. That future is not distant; it is already under construction wherever a single heart chooses patience over pride. Every home that becomes a place of safety, every school that teaches mercy as rigorously as arithmetic, every court that prefers restoration to revenge is a fragment of that coming order. These things seldom reach the news, yet they are the architecture of the possible—the civilization of mercy in embryo.

You may say, *"But the world is still cruel."* Yes—and a garden still contains stones. Yet the soil remembers what has been cleared. The weeds of hatred return more slowly where forgiveness has taken root. Even a small act of mercy alters the climate around it; a single refusal to retaliate cools the temperature of history. If you doubt it, look to the long line of those who refused the sword—Francis of Assisi, Elizabeth Fry, Gandhi, Bonhoeffer, Martin Luther King. Their frailty, multiplied across generations, has bent the arc of power itself. The strong rule for a moment; the gentle rule forever.

The Church, at its best, was meant to be the seedbed of this civilization: not an empire of dogma but a fellowship of the healed. When it forgets and speaks in the accents of coercion, it slips back into the errors of the empires it once redeemed. But when it remembers that its power is persuasion, its logic love, its method service, it becomes again the moral laboratory of the world. Its sacraments are not superstitions but feedback loops of grace—confession, forgiveness, reconciliation—the continual debugging of the human soul.

Outside the sanctuary the same law holds. Politics without mercy hardens into bureaucracy; science without humility decays into hubris; art without truth curdles into vanity. Every institution stands or falls by the kernel's first commandment: *no intentional harm.* When that axiom is broken, decay begins at once; when it is kept, life flourishes as naturally as a vine toward light. The moral and the biological are not two realms but one creation learning to breathe in rhythm.

Imagine, then, what it would mean if the rule of non-coercive good were fully believed. Wars would end not because weapons vanished, but because no heart could justify their use. Markets would measure wealth by generosity; medicine would heal without exploitation; education would prize cooperation over competition. Even our machines would change their purpose, serving creativity instead of appetite. It sounds utopian only because we have forgotten what heaven means—not escape from earth, but earth brought to coherence.

Perhaps that is why Scripture ends not with souls fleeing upward, but with a city descending—Jerusalem remade, the human order purified. The walls remain, for boundaries are eternal, yet the gates stand open all day. No harm may enter—not because guards forbid it, but because no one any longer wishes to harm. The law still stands written, but it has become instinct. The kernel has become character. That is the civilization of mercy completed.

Until that day, we labour as apprentices. Each of us is a small laboratory of moral physics, running experiments in grace. Every choice adds or subtracts from the coherence of creation. To forgive an enemy, to speak truth kindly, to restrain a justified anger—these are not private decencies but maintenance upon the world itself. Every honest word strengthens gravity; every merciful deed repairs the field. We cannot hurry the process by force; we can only consent to it more deeply. For the kernel's boundary is freedom itself—grace moves only at the speed of understanding. Coercion may compel behaviour, but only consent can transform being.

When that consent at last becomes universal, redemption will no longer need to be preached; it will have become the air we breathe. And then—perhaps in a moment no clock can measure—the moral temperature of the universe will reach equilibrium. There will still be motion, but no friction; still choice, but no contradiction. Life will not end; it will at last be safe. The music that began before creation will resolve into its final chord, and the Conductor will rest His hands. Then we shall see that the long agony of history was not wasted but transfigured—that even our worst mistakes were folded into the great lesson of coherence. The world will not be new because the old was destroyed, but because it was at last understood. The kernel will have completed its optimization. The experiment will have succeeded. Love will remain—bounded, yet infinite; humble, yet indestructible—strong enough at last to bear eternity.

Theology as Operating System

The Code of Divine Logic

Every great structure, whether cathedral or cosmos, hides a code. Stone keeps faith with geometry; stars with gravity; even conscience follows an inward syntax that murmurs what ought to be. From the patterned wings of a moth to the equations that bind galaxies, order hums beneath appearance. For centuries theology described that order in the language of heaven while science traced it in the language of matter. Each thought it studied a different realm, yet both were listening to the same rhythm—the quiet architecture that makes reality readable. Call it law, call it Logos, call it the operating system of God.

An operating system never paints the picture on the screen; it makes pictures possible. It is the agreement beneath activity, the protocol that lets chaos cooperate. In that sense, theology has never been the rival of science but its firmware—the logic beneath all logics, the grammar by which being conjugates. When Scripture speaks of the Word through whom all things were made, it names this invisible architecture. John called Him Logos; the mathematician might call Him the kernel of coherence; the poet might simply say light. Every law of physics and every beat of morality runs on that first instruction. The universe is not a random script; it is compiled love.

Before there were alphabets or atoms, there was pattern. In the beginning God did not build; He spoke. Speech implies syntax, syntax implies logic, logic implies faithfulness. The first creation was not matter but meaning—the rule matter would obey, the rhythm in which freedom could safely dance. That rule was love expressed as coherence: no lie could endure, no cruelty remains unbalanced, no rejection be final. Reality was, and still is, the outworking of that code. If theology sounds abstract, it is only because we have forgotten how concrete God's words are when He speaks them. "Let there be light" was not poetry; it was a command line. The light that answered is still executing.

When humanity began to name the Source, it did what every programmer does: it wrote documentation. The early creeds—the Apostles', the Nicene, the Athanasian—were not attempts to imprison mystery but to keep it running. Those antique phrases—substance, person, begotten not made—were system-integrity checks of a faith learning to stay coherent under stress. Each line was written against a specific crash. If Christ were not truly God, salvation would not compile; if love were not free, the universe would deadlock. Doctrine, at its best, was never tyranny but maintenance—the Church running diagnostics on its own understanding. For every great heresy was an unhandled exception. Gnosticism tried to comment out the body; Arianism downgraded divinity; legalism rewrote grace as transaction. The theologians who opposed them were not pedants but engineers defending the integrity of meaning. They knew that bad code executed long enough becomes culture, and culture forms souls.

Yet even perfect systems can fail in one way: when a process demands privileges it was never designed to hold. In moral life, that process is pride. Pride is not self-respect; it is a security breach—the creature attempting root access to the divine kernel without comprehension. The Fall was not merely disobedience; it was the first hack: humanity trying to run the universe in administrator mode. From that moment, history booted into safe mode. Freedom remained, but functionality was throttled. Evil spread like corrupted code replicating across the network.

Instead of wiping the disk and starting fresh, the Architect began a long repair from within—releasing patches through covenants, prophets, conscience, and law. Each update closed another vulnerability of the human spirit. Sin is not only the breaking of rules; it is the breaking of syntax. Comment out "love your neighbour," and the whole program throws errors.

No outside technician could clean this from the periphery. The logic of the system required an inside operation. So the Word became flesh—the Source running inside His own code. This was not mythic theatre but metaphysical surgery: the infinite compiled in a finite process so corruption could be overwritten from the root. In Christ, God showed not merely what love commands, but how love executes—line by line, subroutine by subroutine, obeying the kernel without deviation. The Crucifixion was not a crash; it was a controlled shutdown. The Resurrection was the reboot. At Calvary, the permissions of death were revoked; the obsolete operating system of sin lost compatibility with life. Every resurrection since—of conscience, of culture, of compassion—is a ripple of that original reboot. From that hour the moral universe began migrating to a new build. Decay still hums in background processes, but its code is deprecated. Grace is the current version.

After the reboot comes the long release cycle we call grace. The Holy Spirit is the background process—quiet and persistent—integrating every willing soul into the new build of being. Each prayer is a handshake protocol; each act of forgiveness, a successful merge. Grace is not sentimental pardon but synchronization: the constant reconciliation of heaven's repository with the local copy of the human heart. Repentance, in this light, is simply agreeing to the update. The patches take time to install; they always require consent. No soul is forced to upgrade, yet the invitation never expires. Salvation is not escape from matter but matter patched to perfection—spirit and body running the same version of love.

When the Church remembers itself, it behaves not as a corporation guarding product rights but as an open-source community of co-developers. Every believer is invited to contribute—to write compassion into the world in whatever language their gifts allow. Its creeds are shared documentation; its sacraments are system calls that keep the network alive. Schisms are version conflicts, born not of diversity but of prideful edits unreviewed. Christ did not call His followers an army or a club; He called them a body. In a distributed system one node may fail, yet integrity in the rest can restore it. Communion is redundancy against despair. Each act of reconciliation is data recovery; each act of service, bandwidth shared. Whenever the Church treats grace as proprietary software, it fractures. Whenever it remembers the kernel belongs to all, coherence spreads again.

Even modern science, with all its lenses and accelerators, still runs on faith in coherence. To experiment is to confess that order will answer inquiry—that reason can trust reality's structure. Every laboratory is a small cathedral built on the creed that truth is discoverable. Every true discovery is a modest act of theology: an admission that the universe speaks one language. Revelation, seen from the other side, is research conducted from above. Where science climbs through data, revelation descends through meaning, and they meet midway in coherence. One investigates what the Word has written; the other listens to what the Word is saying. The same Logos writes the stars and the Scriptures. Their harmony is not coincidence; it is signature.

If theology is the operating system, ethics, art, and science are its applications, and their stability depends on kernel integrity. Remove love from politics, and justice freezes. Remove humility from knowledge, and wisdom corrupts. Remove freedom from worship, and holiness curdles into fear. Every cultural collapse is, at bottom, a kernel panic: love's logic has failed beneath the shiny surface of progress. History's revolutions read, in this light, like patch notes. The abolition of slavery was a compatibility fix between dignity and economy. The civil-rights movement was error handling for centuries of racial corruption. Ecological conscience is the system rediscovering resource management. Grace iterates it learns, corrects, persists.

We stand again at a threshold. We are rich in applications and poor in understanding of the kernel. We upgrade devices faster than virtues and automate choices without asking whether they still serve love. The result is speed without direction—systems crashing under the weight of their own efficiency. The task before us is not to reinstall religion as nostalgia but to reboot coherence: to bring every discipline—science, art, governance, markets—back into alignment with the original logic, love plus freedom without rejection. This is not dogma; it is design. The blueprint of redemption runs deeper than culture or creed. The world does not need more religion; it needs a working copy of love.

Imagine universities that teach physics as praise, politics as stewardship, medicine as mercy codified in flesh. Such a civilization would not blur faith and reason; it would fulfill both. The moral algorithm would once again match the physical: compassion efficient, freedom safe, truth beautiful.

At last, Theology as Operating System teaches that creation is not a scatter of miracles but one continuous computation of grace. Every sunrise is the processor clocking another cycle; every prayer a packet sent and received; every act of forgiveness a line successfully compiled. The universe is intelligible because it was spoken, stable because it was loved, redeemable because it was debugged from within. We are not mere users of this system; we are conscious extensions of its logic. And when the last error message fades—when no heart throws exceptions and every mind runs on trust—the interface of heaven will be simple: no icons, no commands, only presence. The code will have become conversation. The operating system and its Maker will be indistinguishable, and coherence complete.

The Heart of Redemption

Why Every Life Matters Beyond Measure

THE DEEPER ONE INVESTIGATES creation, the more personal everything becomes. Numbers turn into faces; laws become stories. Behind every principle of harmony stands a life, and behind every life a will that matters. If love is to be real, no person can be treated as replaceable. That is the secret arithmetic of heaven: there is no such thing as "someone else."

Our age is fluent in measurement—utility, productivity, contribution—as though souls were entries in a ledger. But the gospel whispers another logic: life always comes first. It is what mathematicians would call lexicographic order—you settle the first term completely before moving to the next. Morally, it means that the protection of a single life outranks every calculation of gain. To harm one person for the greater good is to tidy the columns while erasing the name that gives them meaning. Love does not sort lives by size; it alphabetizes them by infinity.

For centuries humanity tried to balance the books of pain—one sacrifice to save many, one war to secure peace, one scapegoat to restore order. The pattern is ancient because it almost works, but it cannot endure. Suffering is not fungible; one agony cannot offset another. Every tear belongs to its own coordinates in eternity. Imagine a symphony in which a wrong note is "cancelled" by striking it louder in another octave: the discord only deepens. The only true correction is resolution, when dissonance is absorbed into harmony without loss of tone. That is what forgiveness does; it ends the note not by ignoring it, but by completing it. Pain cannot be traded; it can only be transfigured.

The heart of redemption declares a single law: no life may be treated as expendable, and no suffering may be treated as exchangeable. Every structure that violates this law eventually collapses. Economies that treat labour as disposable implode; empires that justify conquest decay; even religions that preach sacrifice without empathy lose the melody of their own song. Coherence demands that what is unique be preserved uniquely. If the Redemption Optimization taught that the universe learns, and the Moral Kernel Optimization that it learns without coercion, the heart adds this: it learns without substitution. Love closes wounds directly; it does not outsource them. Justice delegated is justice delayed; mercy delegated is mercy denied.

When Christ said that even the hairs of our head are numbered, He was not describing celestial bookkeeping but divine attention—the refusal to flatten individuality into generality. Heaven's alphabet has no duplicates. That is why forgiveness must be personal: no one can repent for another, and no one can be loved in bulk. In God's dictionary, "neighbour" is not a category but a name waiting to be learned. To love the world truly, one must stop generalizing it.

If suffering cannot be swapped, how is it redeemed? By closure at the place of injury. Forgiveness, restitution, and understanding act locally, like medicine applied to a wound rather than misted into the air. Each reconciliation releases a measure of coherence back into creation. The universe heals person by person, clause by clause. That is why the Incarnation was necessary: divine love could not repair the world from afar; it had to enter the exact coordinate where harm began. Redemption, to be coherent, had to be embodied. The only cure that works everywhere is the one that worked somewhere first.

Abstraction is tidy; it hides the cries. Systems slide into evil the moment they stop hearing individual voices—a prison number replaces a name, a statistic replaces a story, a policy replaces a face—and coherence falters. The heart of redemption warns us: the map is not the mercy. We may reason in generalities, but we must act in particulars. There are no ordinary people; every encounter is with an eternal being. To forget that is to begin the slow amnesia that ends in cruelty. Abstraction kills quietly; it calls the dead "data."

Forgiveness does not erase memory; it redeems it. The wound remains visible, but it no longer bleeds. In the moral physics of the heart, memory is the checksum of coherence: only when pain is remembered rightly can it cease to repeat. To forget too soon is to invite recursion; to remember in love is to achieve closure. Every scar in heaven will tell the same story—harm once existed here, and ended here. Memory without bitterness is eternity's autobiography.

Even our sciences are beginning to notice. Medicine moves from averages to the care of the individual; economics rediscovers dignity through fair trade and honest design; technology learns that privacy and agency are sacred. Each domain, knowingly or not, mirrors the same law: what is unique must remain inviolable. History bends toward coherence not by replacing the weak with the strong, but by teaching strength to guard the fragile. Progress is not faster wheels; it is gentler hands.

The Heart of Redemption is the moral centre of everything that came before it. The Redemption Optimization showed that the universe learns; the Moral Kernel Optimization drew the boundaries of harmlessness; Theology as Operating System revealed the code that runs creation. Now the heart reveals the final constant: each life is a non-fungible proof of love. When this is understood, cruelty loses its last disguise, and compassion ceases to be policy—it becomes perception. To live by this law is to see the world as God sees it: every creature a coordinate of infinite worth, every wound a call for direct repair, every act of love a restoration of syntax in the language of being. Redemption is not arithmetic; it is attention made eternal.

The Coherence of Existence

How Love, Freedom, and Humility Keep the Universe Alive

EVERY STRUCTURE THAT LASTS is held together by something unseen. Atoms keep faith through charge; galaxies through gravity; friendships through trust. Remove that invisible bond and the pattern unravels, however brightly its pieces once shone. The same hidden law sustains existence itself. The universe remains coherent because it rests on three powers working as one—love, freedom, and humility. They are not ornaments of virtue but the load-bearing beams of reality. Take away any one, and creation begins to shake.

Look carefully at any system that endures—an atom, a marriage, a civilization—and you will find the same trinity of relationships: something that draws, something that chooses, something that yields. Physics names them in other tongues—charge, spin, conservation—but the moral geometry is identical. Love draws things together; freedom lets them remain themselves; humility makes their cooperation possible. Without attraction, there is isolation; without freedom, there is tyranny; without humility, there is collapse. These three are the minimal conditions for life, whether biological or spiritual. They are the grammar of relationship itself.

Human history is a commentary on what happens when the equation is unbalanced. Justice without mercy hardens into tyranny. Mercy without truth decays into indulgence. Freedom without love becomes appetite; love without humility turns to control. Each fragment calls itself "the good" and burns out under its own brightness. Partial goodness is the most dangerous force in the world: it burns pure for a moment and then consumes what it meant to protect.

One can even write the pattern, if one dares, as a simple coherence equation: C equals L times F times H—coherence as the product of love, freedom, and humility. Each multiplies the others; when one falls to zero, the whole collapses. A world with love but no freedom becomes a cage; with freedom but no humility, a battlefield; with humility but no love, an empty monastery. Only together do they form the moral kernel—the living engine that keeps reality alive and learning. This is no mystical arithmetic; it is the structure of every stable system. Multiplication, in mathematics, binds independent variables into one expression; in life, love, freedom, and humility bind into coherence. When any term is lost, the equation dissolves. Coherence is not perfection but partnership—the ongoing consent of powers that could dominate and instead choose to harmonize.

Energy in physics can neither be created nor destroyed; it changes form. Moral energy behaves the same way. Love, when blocked, reappears as pain; when expressed, as joy. Hatred is love inverted; despair is faith interrupted. Evil is not a rival force but a leak—the escape of meaning through pride or indifference. Redemption is the sealing of that leak. Every apology, every act of repentance, every humble choice restores moral energy to the system. The heart feels it as peace; communities feel it as trust; the universe records it as rising coherence. Forgiveness is not sentiment; it is conservation. To forgive is to keep charge from draining out of the moral field, to return potential to the circuit of creation. That is why forgiveness feels powerful: it is physics redeemed.

Of the three powers, humility is the quietest and the most decisive. It is gravity for the soul. Without it, love drifts into condescension and freedom into chaos. Humility draws both back toward the center, whispering that greatness is safe only when it bows. The cosmos seems tuned to this law. Stars burn by giving themselves away; rivers carve their power by yielding to gravity; ecosystems thrive more by cooperation than conquest. Everywhere endurance appears, humility is at work. To bow is not to diminish; it is to align with the direction of being. Arrogance breaks under the weight of reality; humility bends and therefore survives. In the language of coherence, humility keeps the system flexible enough to learn; without it, evolution—biological or moral—would stop.

The consequences of imbalance are drearily predictable. When a civilization neglects one element of the triad, decline begins. Pride drains humility; hierarchy replaces service; coercion replaces consent. Then the cascade follows: harm multiplying faster than it can be healed. Empires rise on discipline and fall on arrogance; movements born in compassion wither in self-importance. The moral energy equation never lies; it merely waits to be noticed. History reads like a periodic table of moral chemistry: each nation, each generation, experimenting with proportions of love, freedom, and humility. When the mixture is right, culture flowers; when an element is missing, the reaction turns violent or cold. Pride—counterfeit stability—is the only perpetual-motion machine that never works. It spends energy pretending to create it. No tyranny can last forever; it violates the conservation of coherence.

If this law is true, its traces should shimmer everywhere—and they do. In ecosystems, cooperation outperforms aggression. In psychology, gratitude heals faster than resentment. In politics, humble leadership outlasts charisma. In physics, equilibrium emerges from opposing forces held in conversation. Even the atom is a miniature act of humility: opposite charges orbiting a common centre, neither annihilating the other. Science, without knowing it, keeps rediscovering theology's first formula. What we call progress is simply creation remembering how to behave. Evolution is creation rehearsing virtue.

The same law plays in the small theatre of a single human life. Each of us is a rehearsal of the triad. When love, freedom, and humility meet rightly, we feel whole; when one falters, we fracture. Love without freedom smothers; freedom without humility isolates; humility without love despairs. The spiritual life is not mystical arithmetic but daily calibration—the steady tuning of these three variables until they resonate. To love without smothering is to remember that others are free; to be free without defiance is to remember that truth has boundaries; to be humble without despair is to remember that surrender is alignment, not loss. The saints were not perfect; they were stable. Their coherence outlasted their flaws.

The universe and the soul mirror each other. The macrocosm reveals the laws the microcosm must obey. The orbits of planets and the turnings of conscience share a geometry: attraction moderated by distance, energy held by reverence. Love is gravitational; humility is centripetal; freedom moves in its true orbit when both are present. Together they keep galaxies and hearts from flying apart. This resonance is not coincidence but continuity: the same Word that scripted the atom scripts the conscience. When we act in coherence, we echo the logic that keeps the stars. When we defy it, we create local weather—storms of meaning that must eventually break and clear.

Cultures flourish when they embed the triad in their institutions. Justice works when compassion is yoked to accountability. Economies thrive when enterprise is tethered to humility and the common good. Art endures when it serves beauty rather than vanity. Every failure we call "corruption" is, at root, an imbalance of the equation. Our age suffers from an overdose of freedom and a deficit of humility. We celebrate choice without counting cost. Technology outruns empathy; the world feels powerful but brittle, like a machine running too hot. To restore coherence is not nostalgia; it is maintenance. We must cool the engines with humility, lubricate freedom with love, and reintroduce meaning as the governing code.

All that has come before in this book prepares this synthesis. The Redemption Optimization showed that the universe learns. The Moral Kernel Optimization traced the boundaries of harmlessness. Theology as Operating System revealed the logic beneath law. The Heart of Redemption declared that each life is sacred beyond exchange. Now the coherence of existence binds them together. Love gives direction—the vector of goodness.

Freedom gives motion—the possibility of creation. Humility gives balance—the correction that keeps both true. Together they conserve moral energy across every level of being, from atoms to angels. The result is what Scripture calls eternal life: not endless duration but unbroken coherence. Eternity is not a clock that never stops; it is a harmony that does not fail.

Goodness, then, is not a mood but a structure—the architecture of reality rendered moral. Every act of pride fractures it; every act of humility repairs it. The world endures because, at its heart, God keeps choosing coherence over chaos and invites us to do the same. To sin is to introduce noise. To repent is to tune again to the original pitch. Heaven is not reward for obedience so much as the final stability of love. Hell is not an arbitrary sentence so much as coherence refused a note that will not tune. The laws of eternity are simply the laws of relationship perfected.

When we live within that harmony, we become co-sustainers of existence. Every sincere prayer, every act of mercy, every refusal to retaliate adds tensile strength to the fabric of the world. We are not passive spectators of divine architecture; we are builders within it, apprentices of coherence. God does not only hold creation together from above; He holds it together through every heart that consents to His rhythm. To act justly, to love freely, to walk humbly—these are not chores but cosmic cooperation. They keep the lights on.

Listen, and you can hear it—the pulse of coherence beneath every heartbeat, the whisper in every reconciliation. It is the rhythm that keeps galaxies turning and friendships mending. It is the triune heartbeat of God echoing in creation: love, freedom, humility—three notes, one chord, an endless song. When that song is fully learned, time will have nothing left to teach. Friction will vanish from the fabric; every choice will harmonize with every other. Existence will rest, not from exhaustion but from completion—the quiet, luminous stillness of a universe that finally understands its own music. And the Word who spoke it all will smile, for the code has executed perfectly. Coherence will have become creation's native tongue. Life will not merely continue; it will rejoice.

Aftermath Equations

The Collapse of Evil and the Transfiguration of Love

Part 1—Prelude: The Moral Wavefunction

EVERY ACT OF THOUGHT, every choice of heart, every tremor of will, unfolds within a field of possibility. Reality is not a chain of fixed events but a wave of potential—an immense, shimmering spectrum of what might be, awaiting collapse into what is. Physics first whispered this in its language of quanta, but the moral world has always known it in its own way. Each human soul stands before the branching of time as surely as an electron before the double slit. Until the choice is made, the future remains suspended—a superposition of virtue and betrayal, courage and retreat.

What collapses the wave is not accident but attention. Observation, in the moral realm, is decision. The conscience is the universe's measuring device. It takes the scattered light of possibility and resolves it into the single beam of actuality. When a being endowed with freedom perceives what is right and then acts upon it, the field contracts; the wave resolves; coherence increases. To choose with understanding is to perform a measurement on the fabric of creation.

The moral wavefunction, then, is the sum of all unrealized goods and evils—every branch that could be, still singing in the mind of God. It hums beneath history, a living psalm of potential coherence. When love acts, one of its notes becomes real; when hate acts, a discord enters. The system learns from each vibration. The cosmos, vast beyond comprehension, is not indifferent machinery but the theatre of this learning.

In the beginning, the field was pure: no contradiction, no harm, no noise in the signal of being. Freedom was born, and with it, the first oscillation—the possibility of divergence. Yet even that divergence served purpose. The wave of freedom was permitted to move so that love could prove its strength. A universe without risk would have no meaning; one without recovery would have no mercy. So, the wave expanded. It still expands—each choice a new measurement, each act of understanding a correction of phase.

Mathematically, we might write it this way:

$$\Psi_{moral}(x,t) = \Sigma_i\, a_i\, |E_i\rangle$$

where each $|E_i\rangle$ represents a moral event, a possible branch of action, and each amplitude a_i measures the likelihood of that path being chosen. But these coefficients are not determined by probability alone—they depend on awareness. As consciousness increases, the destructive interference of ignorance diminishes. Love changes the probability field; humility stabilizes it. The observer is never neutral, for every act of attention bends the moral universe toward or away from coherence.

Every sin, then, is a mis-measurement—a collapse into incoherence. Every act of repentance re-opens the waveform, allowing understanding to re-superpose the options until the right one is chosen. Forgiveness, in this sense, is not sentiment but re-computation. It re-enters the system into the field of grace, where all harm can be recalculated into meaning.

The prophets spoke of this in parable; the physicists in symbol. Both told the same story: that existence is participatory. We are not spectators of creation but its operators, each choice a small act of cosmological maintenance. When a person chooses kindness over cruelty, the amplitude of coherence grows. When they choose pride, the phase of meaning shifts, and the moral interference pattern grows darker. Yet the wave never ends—it is only ever corrected.

Thus, evil is not an independent entity; it is noise in the signal of being. It cannot create; it can only distort. And distortion, once identified, can always be repaired. The field itself—what Scripture calls *the Word upholding all things*—retains memory of the original pattern. Through repentance, the waveform remembers its melody. Through grace, it re-tunes.

The moral wavefunction is the story of creation learning to sing in tune again.

It is the pulse behind history, the rhythm beneath every act of love, the breath that animates forgiveness. It does not end in collapse, but in convergence—the great stabilization of meaning when every choice, every lesson, every sorrow has been harmonized into a single chord.

In that day, the function will not vanish; it will resolve. The wave will not flatten into silence; it will rise into music. And the listener will understand at last that it was his own heart, all along, that the universe had been teaching to hear.

Part 2—The Collapse Operator (S^*)

Every universe of freedom must possess a moment of decision, a point where possibility yields to actuality. In physics this is the act of measurement; in the moral world it is the act of will. Between intention and deed lies the instant when the soul observes itself. That instant is the moral equivalent of quantum collapse. The equations may continue to hum in abstraction, but reality changes only when a conscience consents.

The symbol S^* designates that consent—the operator of confirmation. In mathematical shorthand we might write:

$$S^*(\Psi_{moral}) = E^+$$

where Ψ_{moral} is the field of potential actions and E^+ the event that becomes real. Yet behind the algebra stands something infinitely personal: awareness joined to choice. The collapse is not forced from without; it is evoked from within. The observer and the observed are one creature learning to see.

When the heart acts against conscience, it still collapses the field, but into incoherence. The symbol then reverses:

$$S^{\bullet}(\Psi_{moral}) = E^{-}$$

—a contraction into contradiction. The universe registers this as strain, as unbalanced energy in the moral field. We feel it as guilt; history records it as harm. The cosmos is never indifferent; every moral collapse sends a wave through the lattice of being. Harm may localize, but its resonance travels.

Repentance is the reopening of that contraction. It is the act of re-measurement under new light, when the observer confesses that the first reading was false. In human terms it feels like sorrow; in physical terms it is feedback. The field adjusts until the distortion disappears. The same event that once emitted pain now emits instruction. The system has learned.

We may picture it as a sequence:

$$\Psi_{moral} \rightarrow S^{\bullet}E^{-} \rightarrow \text{Understanding} \rightarrow \Psi'_{moral} \rightarrow S^{*}E^{+}$$

Every true redemption follows that path. Nothing is wasted—not even error. The mis-collapse becomes data for the next correction. This is what theologians call grace: that the universe is permitted to re-measure itself until coherence is restored.

To watch this process within oneself is to glimpse divine pedagogy at work. A child lies, and the world darkens a little; he confesses, and light returns. A nation injures another, then repents through reconciliation; the field brightens again. The scales of consequence are vast, yet the operator is the same. Creation keeps testing its own truth until it holds.

At Calvary the pattern reached its critical point. The whole moral wavefunction of history—every failed measurement, every unclosed wound—collapsed upon one consciousness. There the operator S* was enacted in absolute form. Infinite freedom met infinite love and produced coherence that could no longer decay. From that moment, all subsequent collapses could be corrected by reference to it, as smaller oscillations stabilizing around a fixed harmonic. In formal language we might write:

$$S^*_{\text{Cross}}(\Psi_{\text{world}}) = \Psi_{\text{coherent}}$$

But words are better than symbols. The Cross is the point where the universe learned to measure without harming. Observation became compassion; judgment became restoration. The act of seeing no longer destroyed what it examined—it redeemed it.

Since then, every conscience operates as a miniature of that same event. Each moral choice is a local application of S*. To forgive is to collapse anger into understanding. To love freely is to let truth measure desire until it comes into tune. The cosmos has delegated its own maintenance to its inhabitants. The divine algorithm runs through every willing heart.

Thus, S* is not a mystical sigil but a description of the simplest, hardest thing in the world: attention wedded to mercy. To look at reality with love is to make it real in the right way. Nothing less will do. The eye that hates distorts what it sees; the eye that loves perceives truth. "Blessed are the pure in heart," said the Teacher, "for they shall see God"[1]—that is, they shall measure rightly.

And when all measurements agree, when every observer chooses love over fear, the field will no longer need to collapse. It will have stabilized into coherence itself. The observer will have become indistinguishable from the light he beholds.

Part 3—The Genesis Constraint

Every act of creation begins with a limit. Light was not commanded to be everywhere, but to be separated from the dark.

1. Matt 5:8.

The seas were told, "Thus far and no farther."[2] Even life itself was breathed into form only when matter accepted the shape of breath. The first chapters of Genesis are not poems of boundless power but of measured permission. The universe came into coherence through restraint.

Modern thought, enamoured of infinity, often forgets this. We imagine freedom as expansion without edge, power as growth without gravity. Yet the first law written into reality was a boundary condition:

$$\partial\Omega = 0 \text{ for coherence.}$$

In words: coherence requires a closed surface, a definable border through which meaning can circulate without leaking into nothingness. A universe without borders would dissipate like steam; a self without conscience would dissolve into appetite. The same equation governs both.

When the ancients spoke of Eden, they were describing this principle in mythic language. The garden was coherence embodied: life bounded by reverence. The single prohibition—*do not eat*—was not cruelty but calibration. It fixed the moral constant of the system:

$$L \cdot F \cdot H = 1$$

where L stands for Love, F for Freedom, and H for Humility. Each variable could fluctuate, but their product had to remain unity. Break the balance—raise freedom without humility, inflate love without truth—and the equation falls below one; coherence decays. The serpent's whisper, you shall be as gods, was the first suggestion of division by zero.

The fall was therefore not an experiment in knowledge but in ignoring constraint. Humanity touched the limit to see if it still burned. The result was not enlightenment but instability: a moral singularity where meaning could no longer hold. Yet even in that

2. Job 38:11.

breach, the deeper law endured. For every violation produces its own vector of correction; every excess summons the counter-force of mercy. The Genesis Constraint is self-restoring.

In physical terms, creation's stability rests on symmetry breaking followed by restoration. Matter differentiates into particles, then recombines into atoms, then into stars. Each cycle of division and reunion writes the same sentence in another alphabet: separation that returns to harmony. In moral life, sin and forgiveness are those phases. The difference is intention: matter obeys; will must consent.

Here the constraint becomes covenant. To live coherently is to agree that freedom shall never purchase knowledge at the price of love. It is to treat every boundary not as prison but as promise. When the child learns that fire burns, the knowledge does not destroy curiosity; it sanctifies it. The world remains open, but the opening now has rhythm.

We can express this rhythm as a differential:

$$dC/dt = k((dL/dt)FH + L(dF/dt)H + LF(dH/dt))$$

where C is coherence and k a constant of grace. The equation states that coherence changes not by any single virtue alone, but by their mutual growth. Increase one and the others must respond or the whole declines. This is the moral analogue of conservation of energy: goodness can neither be created nor destroyed, only transferred among its forms.

The prophets saw this long before the calculus existed. "He hath shewed thee, O man, what is good,"[3] wrote Micah; "to do justly, and to love mercy, and to walk humbly with thy God." Justice, mercy, humility—three terms, one invariant. The Genesis Constraint is older than mathematics; mathematics merely rediscovers it.

Every civilization that endures rediscovers it too. Empires fall when freedom forgets humility, when the will of the strong crosses the derivative of love into negative slope. But even their

3. Mic 6:8.

ruin teaches. The ashes record the boundary in clearer ink. Rome's collapse wrote *remember measure* across the ages; the cross of Christ wrote it in light.

The constraint is not punitive. It is protective. It ensures that learning does not annihilate the learner. The forbidden fruit was not knowledge itself but unbounded knowledge—the attempt to read the source code without reverence. To this day, the same temptation whispers through our sciences and our politics: knowledge without humility, progress without proportion. Each time, the correction waits patiently in the wings. Reality, like a good teacher, allows experiment but not final incoherence.

Thus, the Genesis Constraint is the first mercy. It keeps freedom from imploding under its own gravity. It is the quiet law behind every commandment, every conscience, every natural limit that says "enough." And when the universe is finally mature enough to obey it not by compulsion but by comprehension, the constraint will no longer feel like rule but rhythm—the pulse of a creation that has learned how to love without harm.

Part 4—The Feedback of Redemption

Every system that lives must be able to correct itself. A heart that cannot adjust its rhythm dies; a planet without ecological feedback burns or freezes; a conscience that cannot repent turns to stone. Creation endures because it listens to the sound of its own imbalance and answers. This answering—this ceaseless conversation between deviation and restoration—is what Scripture calls redemption and science calls feedback.

The simplest circuit may teach the holiest lesson. A thermostat does not banish cold; it reads it and responds. Grace works by the same logic. It does not erase the consequence of error but turns it into signal. Every moral act, like every flow of current, produces information about its harmony or its distortion. That information does not vanish; it travels until it finds an instrument humble enough to translate it into understanding. Thus, the universe learns by confession.

We can express this learning as a recurrence relation:

$$E_{t+1} = E_t - \alpha \nabla H(E_t)$$

where E_t is the moral error at time t, H the harm function, and α the step of grace. Each act of mercy lowers the gradient; each repetition of cruelty increases it. If $\alpha \to 1$, understanding converges, and the residual harm E_t approaches zero. In words: when grace equals courage, suffering becomes instruction, not destiny.

History has always written this equation with blood. A war reveals the folly of vengeance, and nations swear "never again." The oath breaks, the cycle repeats, the correction strengthens. The amplitude of cruelty diminishes with every recurrence. The half-life of hatred shortens. We call it progress when seen in centuries; we call it repentance when felt in a single heart. Both are the same feedback running at different scales.

At the center of the moral circuit stands the Cross—the resonant feedback node of creation. All preceding errors were summed there, all gradients computed, all corrections applied. Infinite freedom met infinite love, and the derivative of pain became zero:

$$(dH/dt)|_{Cross} = 0$$

The system did not halt; it stabilized. Since that moment, the world has been learning under a new constant. Every act of forgiveness aligns with that equilibrium; every cruelty opposes it. But the equilibrium holds; its value cannot decay. The blood that once dripped as suffering now circulates as understanding.

Forgiveness, in this light, is not a moral luxury but a thermodynamic necessity. Without it, the moral field overheats. Anger accumulates energy faster than compassion can dissipate it. To forgive is to restore balance—to convert potential harm into kinetic learning. That is why peace feels lighter: entropy has been reduced. Every apology is a release valve in the system of being.

And the feedback is reciprocal. Those who grant mercy are healed as surely as those who receive it. For when love answers harm, it closes the open circuit that pain had left behind. The current of coherence flows again, and both poles—offender and offended—glow with the same charge. This is why vengeance darkens both and forgiveness brightens both; the equation is symmetrical. Justice without grace is direct current with no return path: it burns out the wire.

We may think of redemption, therefore, not as miracle but as maintenance. The universe is not a machine to be wound once and abandoned; it is a living instrument tuned continually. The psalmist called it "He restoreth my soul."[4] The engineer might call it negative feedback; the poet, mercy; the saint, love remembering itself. All three are true.

Each of us participates in this great regulation. To repent is to update the model; to forgive is to propagate the correction. The church, at its best, is the world's calibration laboratory. Confession measures the deviation; absolution resets the baseline. Outside the sanctuary, the same law governs politics, ecology, friendship. A policy that cannot admit error cannot improve; a river that cannot overflow its banks cannot renew its soil; a soul that cannot weep cannot learn. Feedback is not weakness but wisdom—the humility of power in conversation with truth.

The culmination of feedback is harmony. When every error has been heard and answered, when no harm remains unacknowledged, the system will no longer oscillate. It will hum at rest—motion without friction, change without loss. Then $E_t = 0$ for all $t > T_f$: the final convergence. Theologians call that heaven; physicists might call it steady-state coherence. It is the same reality described in two dialects.

Until that day, redemption continues as iteration. Each act of patience is another step toward stability, each kindness another data point of grace. The algorithm is slow because freedom is respected. God will not accelerate comprehension by force; understanding must grow at the speed of consent. But the direction is certain, for the derivative of love is always positive.

4. Ps 23:3.

When at last the feedback loop closes entirely—when every echo of pain has been answered by understanding—the song of creation will resolve on its final chord. There will still be rhythm but no recoil, motion but no waste. And in that stillness we shall know that every correction was compassion in disguise, every scar a solved equation. The universe will have learned what it was made to learn: that love is the only stable state.

Part 5—The Equilibrium of Heaven

Every equation that truly converges ends in stillness. Not the stillness of death, but of balance—motion continuing without waste, energy flowing without friction. In such a state, nothing is cancelled; everything is fulfilled. The universe itself seems to be striving toward that condition, as if the whole of creation were solving for rest. Scripture names that rest *Sabbath*. Physics calls it *equilibrium*. Theology calls it *heaven*.

Equilibrium does not mean sameness. It means that every force finds its counterpart, every tension its complement. In formal terms we might write:

$$\nabla L^* = 0 \Rightarrow F^* = -\nabla L^*$$

The gradient of love is zero; freedom flows as its harmonic field. This is not mysticism; it is the final law of coherence. When love and freedom are perfectly differentiated yet perfectly aligned, the moral potential ceases to oscillate. The field has found its home.

We have felt moments of that equilibrium, brief and dazzling, when desire and duty, thought and affection, act and consequence fall into one motion. The musician at the height of performance, the surgeon in focused compassion, the mother watching her child sleep—all know what it is to move without inner division. In that instant, the will and the world rhyme. That is a foretaste of heaven: coherence experienced locally in time.

The saints described it differently, for language bends under joy. They called it peace that passes understanding[5], the rest of God, the union of the soul. Yet the pattern is the same across all vocabularies: a state where all feedback has resolved, where no correction remains unmade. The derivative of harm is not merely small; it is null:

$$dH/dt = 0$$

The moral temperature has stabilized; the universe has reached thermal rest in love.

Heaven, then, is not elsewhere but else-*when*: the completion of the process begun in matter and conscience alike. It is not an interruption of nature but its perfection. The laws of physics are not abolished; they are baptized. Entropy, once feared as decay, becomes the proof that only coherence endures. Everything unstable burns itself away; what remains is indestructible precisely because it no longer resists the law that made it.

This is why eternal life is not endless duration but unbroken harmony. Time, as we know it, is the interval between cause and correction. When every cause corrects itself at once—when love and freedom coincide perfectly—time will flatten into song. The motion will continue, but without delay. To live eternally is to move at the speed of understanding.

In such a world, the commandments will still exist, but as instincts. The law will be written on the heart because the heart will have become lawful. Choice will remain, but every choice will harmonize with the whole, as every note in a perfect chord supports the others. Freedom will not vanish; it will finally be safe. The creature will desire only what the Creator desires, not by decree but by comprehension. That is the equilibrium of heaven.

The mathematician may picture it as convergence to a fixed point:

$$x_{t+1} = f(x_t), \text{ with } x_{t+1} = x_t = x^*$$

5. Phil 4:7.

The theologian would say: the will of man has become one with the will of God. Both sentences describe the same reality—the disappearance of recoil.

And what, then, becomes of pain? It does not cease to exist as memory, but as accusation. Like a scar that no longer hurts, suffering in the equilibrium of heaven becomes history transfigured. Its data remain, but the signal has been re-encoded. What once screamed "loss" now whispers "learned." The mathematics of mercy preserve every value but change its sign:

Negation becomes affirmation. The ledger closes not by deletion but by transformation.

$$H- \rightarrow -H+$$

When that state arrives, the language of necessity will retire. "It is finished" will be the final theorem of the cosmos. Evil will have no recurrence because ignorance will have no habitat. The feedback loops of redemption will fall silent, not from exhaustion but from success. And the Creator, who has laboured since the first dawn to teach His creation coherence, will rest—not alone, but among beings who now understand what rest means.

In that rest there will still be laughter, discovery, creation. Infinity will remain infinite; curiosity will remain holy. But there will be no fear in the search, for all seeking will begin and end in love. Every experiment will glorify its subject; every new world will echo the first sentence of Genesis, now understood completely: *Let there be light.*

The last law will therefore be simple enough for a child to recite and profound enough to hold eternity:

$$L \cdot F \cdot H = 1$$

Love, Freedom, and Humility multiplied remain coherence entire. The equation of creation will at last describe its fulfilment. The universe will hum in that constant; the redeemed will breathe it. And the song that began before atoms were born will continue, unchanged but unending—

Love as law, Freedom as form, Humility as forever.

Part 6—The Genesis of Grace

Every truth that endures must learn to dwell in dust. Heaven's symmetry, if it is to be more than vision, must find form in time. And so, grace descends—not as thunder or decree, but as habit. The eternal law $L \cdot F \cdot H = 1$ begins to translate into the slow syntax of mortal days: love expressed in labour, freedom practiced in patience, humility taught by error. The perfection of heaven, seen through the prism of human frailty, refracts into duty, art, friendship, governance, healing. This refraction is the genesis of grace—the long unfolding of coherence within history.

> Grace begins not as privilege but as pressure relieved.
>
> A man who forgives has broken the ancient chain of retaliation; a woman who tells the truth though it costs her has stopped the entropy of deceit.
>
> Such acts look small, but they are tectonic in the moral crust of the world.
>
> Every forgiveness alters the field.
>
> Every kindness redistributes tension.

The gradient of harm decreases by a measurable amount:

$$\Delta H < 0 \Rightarrow \Delta C > 0$$

where H is harm and C is coherence. Grace is the only energy known to grow by being given away. Unlike power, which divides when shared, grace multiplies. A single act of mercy can echo through a family for generations; a single refusal to hate can reroute the course of nations. This multiplication is not metaphor but arithmetic in another key:

$$G_{t+1} = G_t(1 + \beta)$$

where β is the reproduction rate of mercy. Every act of understanding raises the constant; every resentment lowers it. The moral population of the world, measured in grace, grows by contact.

> To live by grace, then, is to conduct cosmic energy at human scale.
>
> Hospitals are its laboratories; schools are its training grounds; homes are its temples.
>
> Whenever the sick are healed without exploitation, whenever knowledge is shared without vanity, whenever love serves without coercion, the equilibrium of heaven touches the ground.
>
> Civilization, at its best, is grace institutionalized.
>
> Law without mercy petrifies; art without humility corrupts; science without reverence blinds.
>
> But when all three meet—when love, freedom, and humility enter the same sentence—society becomes sacrament.
>
> The kingdom of God appears not as invasion but as integration.

History itself can be read as a set of grace events. Each reform, each awakening, each rediscovery of conscience is another iteration of heaven's algorithm.

> Slavery outlawed, women honoured, enemies reconciled—each is a solved equation in the long problem of love.
>
> The pattern is recursive: every generation inherits an error term and must minimize it.

Some converge faster than others, but the trajectory is fixed:

$$\lim_{t \to \infty} H(t) = 0$$

Grace is not a poet's indulgence, nor a theologian's ornament, but the plainest fact written in the very grain of the world. It is not sentiment but law—not a mood of heaven but its method. The evidence is before us, if only we will read it: cruelty exhausts itself, compassion gathers power, understanding spreads like light along a ridge at dawn. The struggle between coherence and chaos is not merely moral; it is biological. In every corner of creation the same pattern asserts itself. The creatures that devour soon perish; the creatures that cooperate endure. Empires of tooth and claw burn out, while humble colonies and patient partnerships thrive. Even in the field and the forest, heaven rehearses its logic.

And yet grace remains a delicate thing, for it cannot be commanded. You may drive obedience with fear, but you cannot drive love. You may compel silence, but never song. Grace blooms only where it is chosen; it cannot be summoned by rule or forced by power. No algorithm will yield it, no empire can enforce it, for grace is freedom learning what to do with itself. That is why coercion, however well-intentioned, cannot bring heaven to earth. The will must want the law for the law to live.

The patience of God, so often mistaken for neglect, is only the courtesy of love waiting for comprehension. He does not shout what can be whispered, nor strike what may be shown. Grace teaches by invitation, not intrusion; by illumination, not intimidation. That is why it seems slow—it waits for the pupil's eyes to open. But once they do, the lesson cannot be forgotten.

For understanding, once seen, does not unsee itself. Mercy, once learned, cannot be unlearned. Truth, once grasped, is never willingly released. Like a melody remembered after the words have faded, grace continues to hum beneath our thoughts. We may resist it, but resistance itself decays. Pride is a short-lived energy, burning hot and brief; humility endures, and therefore wins. Hatred spends itself quickly; kindness replenishes as it gives. This asymmetry is not accident—it is the architecture of reality. The universe itself seems tilted toward grace, as though God, in the act of creating, gave the whole machinery of being a secret bias toward mercy. The very laws of motion lean toward kindness; the grain of reality runs one way, and that way is love. Even the moral mathematics confess it:

$$dE_{evil}/dt < 0, dE_{good}/dt \geq 0$$

Evil burns itself out as it moves; good gathers strength by doing. Pride is an unstable element—it flares and collapses. Hatred, like friction, turns its own energy into heat and vanishes into waste. But love, like light, multiplies by reflection. It endures because it gives; it expands because it yields. Entropy drains cruelty; coherence conserves love. The fabric of the world itself is moral—it unravels what wounds and preserves what heals.

And so, the meek shall inherit the earth[6]—not by cunning, not by conquest, but simply by endurance. Power runs down; gentleness runs deep. The great experiment of history is proving this with quiet precision. Grace is not an event that interrupts the natural order—it is the natural order discovered at last.

The genesis of grace, therefore, is not a sudden dawn but a slow sunrise. It advances through the centuries as light advances through fog—each age a little brighter than the one before. From a distance the change is plain to see: what began as terror becomes trust; what began as thunder becomes understanding. The commandments that once echoed from Sinai now whisper within conscience. The sacrifice that once demanded blood becomes gratitude that offers praise. The law that once frightened becomes the language of love.

Religion itself matures from transaction to transformation. The altar becomes table; the victim becomes guest. Humanity, long haunted by fear of God, begins to recognize His likeness in one another. The chasm between heaven and earth narrows with every act of mercy. Grace does not abolish nature—it fulfils it. It is creation learning its own design, until love, freedom, and humility (that sacred equation $L \cdot F \cdot H = 1$) are not doctrines to recite but instincts to breathe. The formula becomes flesh. The law becomes life.

6. Matt 5:5.

And when that recognition is complete—when every eye can look upon another and see, not enemy nor stranger, but the image of the Creator—the circle will close, and history will cease to be tragedy. The long feud between command and comprehension will end; what was once obedience will become understanding. The veil between reason and worship will fall away, and knowledge will kneel of its own accord.

Then, as the last echo of resistance fades, the earth will breathe with the same rhythm as heaven. Every institution will mirror that music; every heart will join the choir. Science will become doxology; justice will sound like mercy; beauty will no longer apologize for truth. The whole world will have learned what heaven has always known—that grace is simply the logic of love applied.

In that hour, creation will remember its name. The equations will rest, not because they fail, but because they are finished. What began in law will end in life. What began in time will end in meaning. And the universe, having learned mercy through its long schooling of pain, will rise at last as one great act of comprehension—an eternal thought in the mind of God, perfectly coherent, perfectly free, perfectly humble.

Part 7—The Architecture of the New World

When the last discord is resolved, creation will not fall silent. It will begin again—only now in tune. The song that once climbed through centuries of sorrow will return as harmony, not lament. Yet this new world will not appear by miracle from the sky; it will grow from within the old, as order grows from seed. The Kingdom of Heaven is not a fortress descending upon the earth, but a structure rising through it—the slow crystallization of grace into form.

Look first to the smallest things, for that is where the foundation is laid. A single home where anger yields to patience is already the architecture of the new world. A teacher who corrects without humiliation, a judge who seeks restoration more than revenge, a merchant who measures wealth by fairness rather than gain—these are cornerstones. The blueprints of eternity are drafted in the gestures of an ordinary day. Every institution that learns mercy adds a pillar; every honest conversation adds a window. Cathedrals of policy and science will follow later; the walls of the heart must rise first.

The world that emerges from coherence will not glitter with novelty but glow with understanding. Technology will remain, yet its purpose will change: no longer the amplification of appetite, but the extension of compassion. Machines will serve creativity instead of covetousness; knowledge will flow not for power but for participation. In such a society the word *progress* will regain its innocence—it will mean not acceleration but alignment.

Justice will move from punishment to prevention, from balance sheets of guilt to the quiet arithmetic of repair. Law will still exist, but it will have changed its tense. Instead of saying, "You must not," it will say, "You need not." Education will no longer train competitors but awaken collaborators, minds taught to think in harmonies rather than hierarchies. The arts will abandon despair as a badge of depth and rediscover praise as a discipline of vision. And theology, having translated heaven into coherence, will find its own perfection in gratitude.

Such transformation will not erase struggle; it will transfigure it. The world will still move, but its motion will be music. Labor will remain, but toil will have gone. Death itself will not vanish; it will have become transparent—another word for passage, not annihilation. The entire creation will breathe in one rhythm: Love as law, Freedom as pulse, Humility as balance. The great equation—$L \cdot F \cdot H = 1$—will no longer be written in books but in behaviour. It will be the grammar of existence, learned by instinct, spoken by every living thing.

In that age, faith will not argue; it will demonstrate. Reason will not dissect; it will delight. The scientist and the saint will work side by side, one tracing the mathematics of mercy, the other its music. Every discovery will be an act of worship, every prayer a research of the heart. The schism between mind and spirit will close like a healed wound. Knowledge will once again be praise articulated.

This, then, is the architecture of the new world: not towers of triumph but a city of tenderness. Its walls will still stand, for boundaries are eternal, but its gates will never shut. No guard will forbid entry, for nothing within desires to harm. Authority will not disappear; it will be trust made visible. The law will remain, but it will no longer command; it will invite. The last empire will be community itself—a fellowship of the coherent.

Part 8—The Music of Completion

When coherence at last becomes the habit of creation, history will not end—it will mature. Time will continue to flow, but it will flow like melody rather than machinery. The ages will still turn, but not in struggle; each century will become a stanza of one unfolding hymn. The story will no longer move toward resolution—it will *be* resolution. Every act will rhyme with every other; meaning will have become atmosphere.

We shall not wake into another world, but into this one made transparent. The old hills will stand, but their silence will sound like praise. The rivers will still run, but they will seem to know where they are going. Work will remain, but it will feel like worship in motion. And the smallest kindness—a hand steadying another, a truth spoken without pride—will glow with the same quiet splendour as a sunrise.

The difference will not be in what happens, but in how it happens. Choice will still exist, but contradiction will not. The will and the law will have learned to walk together. The commandment will have become comprehension, the covenant, conversation. Love will have found its equilibrium, and freedom its fulfilment. The formula once written in symbol—L · F · H = 1—

will now be the instinct of every heart, the grammar of existence itself. It will not need to be proved; it will be breathed.

In that clarity, all opposites will be reconciled. Knowledge will kneel; faith will stand; worship and work will become the same gesture. Heaven will not hover above the world like a crown; it will pulse through it like a heartbeat. To see a face will be to see

God; to understand anything fully will be to love it. The distinction between sacred and secular will fade, not by loss but by fulfilment, as daylight renders lamps unnecessary.

And we shall remember the long story behind us—the wars, the grief, the endless learning—and see that none of it was wasted. Every sorrow will appear as a training of sight, every loss, a refinement of love. Pain, which once seemed an accusation, will reveal itself as apprenticeship. The wounds of history will remain visible, but transfigured, like the scars in the risen Christ—proof not of failure, but of fidelity.

Then the Word who spoke the first light will speak again, not to begin but to bless. Creation will answer, not in language but in harmony. The mathematics of mercy will have finished their computation; every variable reconciled; every fraction of fear reduced to zero. The universe will rest—not the stillness of exhaustion, but the poise of understanding.

And we shall know what all the centuries were about. Not conquest, not survival, not progress for its own sake, but coherence—the slow realization that love was the structure of reality from the first and freedom its necessary proof. The lesson will be complete, and the Teacher will need to speak no more.

Then there will be silence, and in that silence—music. A single note, steady as eternity, sustaining everything that lives:

the sound of a universe that has learned how to love.

Part III: The Gospel of Coherence

The Word and the World

Creation—The Language of Being

IN THE BEGINNING WAS not matter but meaning. Before the first atom turned or the first light broke, there was a Voice. "In the beginning was the Word (Logos), and the Word was with God, and the Word was God."[1] All that would ever exist began as articulation. Creation is not an accident of physics but the utterance of intelligence, the music of an infinite mind made audible in space and time.

The ancients felt this long before they could name it. The Hebrew poets spoke of Dabar YHWH—the Word of the Lord—as a living agent: "By the word of the Lord the heavens were made, and by the breath of His mouth all their host."[2] To them, speech and spirit were twins; breath carried both. The Greeks, listening from another shore, called it Logos: not merely a word spoken but the principle that makes speech possible—the inner reason of reality.

Thus when John begins his Gospel with *Logos*, he gathers the wisdom of both worlds and fuses them. He tells us that the logic scientists seek in equations and the order philosophers seek in reason are already one in the eternal Son. Every constant in the cosmos—gravity's curve, light's velocity, the precision of hydrogen's bond—is a syllable in that divine syntax.

1. John 1:1–3.

2. Ps 33:6.

To study creation is therefore to overhear God thinking aloud. The galaxies are not chaotic; they are grammatical. They move according to verbs of relation: attraction and release, rotation and rest. Even in their collisions there is choreography. What physics calls symmetry, theology calls faithfulness—the refusal of reality to break its own covenant.

When modern eyes peer through telescopes or particle accelerators, they are reading the same Word in another script. The psalmist had already said it: "Day unto day pours forth speech, and night unto night reveals knowledge."[3] Creation is fluent; it never stops talking. The scientist, the artist, and the saint are all translators of the same sentence, each rendering a fragment of the original into human tongue.

And what is that sentence? Love. Not the sentiment, but the structure. "God is love" (1 John 4:8), writes the apostle—not *has* love, but *is* it. To say that God is love is to say that relationship is older than substance. Being itself is communion. That is why every durable thing in the universe—molecule, marriage, or melody—survives only through harmony. The coherence of the cosmos is the outward form of love's inward grammar.

Incarnation—The Word Made Flesh

Yet words, however beautiful, are not complete until they are heard. The Logos that shaped the stars desired to be understood from within its own creation. So "The Word became flesh and dwelt among us, and we have seen His glory, glory as of the only Son from the Father, full of grace and truth."[4]

Here the Author writes Himself into His own story. The infinite enters the finite not as a thunderclap but as a heartbeat. The same voice that once commanded galaxies now cries in a manger. The grammar of God takes on human grammar; omniscience learns to speak in syllables.

3. Ps 19:2.
4. John 1:14.

Why? Because comprehension requires proximity. A truth shouted from heaven might compel awe but not love. So the Word descends into the density of flesh to translate divinity into the dialect of empathy. "Though He was in the form of God, He did not count equality with God a thing to be grasped, but emptied Himself" (Phil 2:6–7). The humility that binds atoms together now binds itself in swaddling cloth.

The Incarnation is not a footnote to creation; it is its fulfillment. For creation was always meant to be conversational—a dialogue between Maker and made. "Let us make man in our image," said God (Gen 1:26), as though love could not be content until it had a counterpart who could answer. In Christ, that conversation becomes audible again. Humanity hears its own language spoken without distortion for the first time since Eden.

Every miracle, every parable, every act of forgiveness in the Gospels is a restoration of syntax. When Jesus heals the leper, He is correcting a misspelled line in the poem of creation. When He forgives the adulteress, He is closing a parenthesis that sin had left open. Each gesture re-teaches the world its native grammar of mercy.

Then comes the Cross—the point where the Word meets the world at its most incoherent. There, language itself seems to fail. The sentence breaks: "My God, My God, why hast Thou forsaken Me?"[5] But even that cry is quotation; He is speaking the psalm that foretold His suffering. Meaning is not lost—it is descending to the depth of meaninglessness to rescue it.

The theologians call this *atonement*, but the older English was more precise: *at-one-ment*—the making of oneness. At Calvary, the divine subject bears the full predicate of creation's pain. He who spoke coherence into being absorbs its negation so that the sentence may continue. The nails that pierce His hands fasten the torn pages of existence back together.

When He says, "It is finished,"[6] the phrase is not despair but notation. The Word that once said "Let there be light" now declares

5. Matt 27:46; Ps 22:1.

6. John 19:30.

"Let there be forgiveness." The verb changes, but the power is the same. Creation and redemption are two chapters of one grammar—the grammar of grace. Through Him, as Paul writes, "God was pleased to reconcile all things to Himself, making peace through the blood of His cross" (Col 1:20).

From that hill the logic of the universe radiates outward again. The moral field stabilizes; coherence re-enters history as possibility. Where once commandments thundered from stone, now compassion breathes from flesh. Sinai becomes Calvary; law becomes life.

Recognition—The Light That Learns

Still the story continues, for comprehension must be shared. The Word that entered one body now speaks through many. "You are the body of Christ, and individually members of it."[7] Each soul becomes a syllable in the continuing revelation. The divine coherence disperses itself like seeds into soil. "The light shines in the darkness, and the darkness has not overcome it."[8]

This is why grace advances by consent, not command. God could have coerced understanding, but that would have destroyed the freedom that makes love possible. So He teaches instead of forcing. The Spirit interprets what the Son has said, translating it into the languages of conscience, culture, and time. Revelation continues not as new information but as deepened recognition.

Each generation hears again the first sentence of Genesis, this time in its own accent. Science, art, and ethics are the world's attempts to pronounce that sentence correctly. Sometimes the tone is wrong, sometimes the words are reversed, yet the longing remains unmistakable—to speak in harmony with the original Word. "The whole creation groans in labour pains until now," writes Paul (Rom 8:22), because it is still learning its lines.

7. 1 Cor 12:27.

8. John 1:5.

To live coherently, then, is not to escape the world but to participate in its rehearsal. Every act of forgiveness, every patient labor of understanding, is a rehearsal of heaven's final speech. When we love our enemies, we echo the syntax of Calvary; when we create beauty, we replay the overture of Genesis. Even our failures contribute to the learning, for confession is truth rediscovered.

In this light, faith and reason cease to be rivals. They are the two eyes by which the soul perceives depth. Reason traces the pattern; faith trusts the pattern-maker. Together they reveal a world intelligible because it is beloved. The same Logos that structures mathematics structures mercy. "The heavens declare the glory of God," says the psalmist (Ps 19:1); and the Beatitudes declare the same glory translated into human conduct. "Blessed are the meek," for meekness is how gravity feels inside a heart.

The coherence of existence, then, is not an abstract formula but a lived relation. To sin is to speak out of tune with the Word; to repent is to rejoin the melody. The Church, when faithful, is a choir of such re-tuned instruments, each voice correcting the others until harmony returns. When Christ prayed "that they may all be one" (John 17:21), He was not asking for uniformity but for resonance—the music of freedom kept in time by love.

Look around and the evidence appears everywhere. In the patient nurse, the honest judge, the child who comforts a weeping friend—the grammar of God resurfaces. Evil still makes noise, but it is losing its rhythm. History's melody is modulating toward resolution. As John's Gospel opened with "In the beginning," so Revelation closes with "Behold, I make all things new" (Rev 21:5). The first word and the last are the same act of speech—the same coherence rediscovered at a higher octave.

One day, language itself will rest. Theology will become transparency; science, worship; philosophy, praise. Knowledge and love will no longer alternate but coincide. "Now we see through a glass darkly; then face to face" (1 Cor 13:12). When that hour arrives, the universe will not need another explanation, for explanation will have turned into experience. Every law will reveal its lawgiver by resemblance.

Until then, our task is not to invent new truths but to remember the old one—to trace the grammar of grace through the sentences of history. The Word still speaks through the medium of mercy, and the world, though often deafened by its own noise, still vibrates to His tone. Every reconciliation, every act of humility, every quiet choosing of good over gain, is a faint but faithful echo of that first divine syllable: *Let there be light.*

Therefore, the Gospel of Coherence begins here, where faith meets physics, where the eternal Word converses with the temporal world. Creation was never silent; it has been singing all along. The melody only sounds strange to ears that have forgotten the tune. But listen long enough—in the hum of stars, the logic of conscience, the laughter of children—and you will hear it again: the voice that called everything from nothing and still calls everything toward love.

The Fall and the Freedom to Learn

THERE IS A STORY older than time yet still unfolding inside every conscience—the story of how freedom first met love and failed to trust it. Scripture names it *the Fall*, but the word can mislead. We imagine a tumble down some celestial stairway, an accident in Eden. Yet the Bible's tone is more solemn than tragic. It speaks of awakening: of eyes opened too soon, of a question asked before understanding was ready to hold the answer. The serpent's whisper, "Did God really say . . . ?", was not the birth of curiosity but of suspicion. In that moment, freedom turned its face away from love and began to learn by pain.

The garden is not geography but memory. Each soul reenacts its drama: the invitation to trust, the lure to test. "Perhaps the rule no longer applies," we murmur, reaching again for the fruit that promises autonomy. The taste is sweet for a heartbeat, then bitter with knowledge. What Adam and Eve discovered that day was not power but feedback. They touched the flame and learned what fire does to flesh. The wages of sin were not inflicted; they were inherent. Reality itself replied, *You cannot break coherence without being broken by it.*

Yet even here, grace was already at work. God's first question to the hiding pair—"Where are you?"—is not thunder but searchlight. The Creator of galaxies walks in the cool of the evening calling for His children as though ignorance could belong to Him. He asks not because He lacks knowledge, but because they lack courage to step into it. The question is mercy disguised as pursuit. Before judgment is pronounced, dialogue begins again.

Thus, the lesson of the Fall is not merely disobedience but pedagogy. Freedom, newly conscious of itself, collides with consequence and begins to comprehend moral gravity. The expulsion from Eden is not exile so much as enrolment. "By the sweat of your brow you shall eat bread"—not vengeance, but curriculum. The ground that yields thorns becomes the first classroom of cause and effect. Pain enters as tutor, not tyrant.

Paul will later name this schooling: "Through one man sin entered the world, and death through sin; and so death spread to all men, because all sinned." (Rom 5:12) Here death is not a cosmic punishment but the visible shape of moral entropy—the loss of coherence echoing through creation. Yet Paul also perceives the hidden symmetry: "Where sin increased, grace abounded all the more" (Rom 5:20). The system contains its own remedy. The law that exposes failure becomes the light that guides correction. Every fall carries within it the data of its repair.

This, then, is the secret the universe has been learning since Eden: evil is necessary only once. The first dissonance teaches the cost of dissonance; repetition becomes incoherence. The Fall was the single experiment that need never be repeated. What began as tragedy is redeemed as comprehension. Even the curse becomes curriculum—entropy permitted until empathy matures. The prophets discerned this when they heard God promise a new covenant "not like the one made with their fathers," but written "on their hearts" (Jer 31:33). The external command would evolve into internal coherence. Humanity, once expelled from the garden, would become the garden's restoration in miniature—each soul a plot of ground learning again to bear fruit without violation.

Romans 8 reaches further: "The whole creation has been groaning in labor pains until now." The cosmos itself participates in this moral education. Earthquakes, extinctions, and wars are not random spasms but the contractions of a world learning to give birth to understanding. Paul's language is maternal: suffering is travail, not terminal disease. "Creation waits with eager longing for the revealing of the sons of God"—that is, for beings mature enough in love to steward freedom without harm.

Freedom, you see, is the most dangerous gift because it carries God's likeness. To make a creature capable of love, He must also make it capable of rejection. Coercion could have prevented sin, but it would have prevented worship too. Love that cannot say *no* is not love but programming. And so the Father risked the heartbreak of autonomy in order to raise children, not puppets. The cross was already implicit in the breath that gave Adam life.

This divine risk is not recklessness but trust. God believes in what He made. "You will be like gods, knowing good and evil," the serpent promised. It was half true. Humanity would indeed come to know, but by the long road of consequence. To *know* good and evil is not merely to define them but to experience their divergence. The story of civilization is that knowledge in motion: every empire, an essay on what happens when freedom forgets humility. Yet history also shows the feedback working—laws written after injustice, compassion rising after cruelty. The data curve bends toward coherence because reality itself resists sustained contradiction.

Even nature participates in the parable. A bone broken and set properly heals stronger at the fracture. Forests reborn after fire grow richer soil. So too the soul: repentance is the scar turned into strength. The risen Christ bears wounds not erased but glorified. Redemption does not delete history; it transfigures it. "Behold, I make all things new"—not *other*, but *new*: the same material re-written in a better tense.

The Necessary-Once theorem therefore finds its purest image in Calvary. There, the pattern of Eden reverses. A tree again stands at the center of the world. A choice is offered. This time the fruit is obedience, and the garden is Golgotha. Where one man grasped, another yields. "As by one man's disobedience many were made sinners, so by one man's obedience many will be made righteous" (Rom 5:19). The symmetry is astonishing: the first Adam reaching upward to seize divinity; the second Adam descending to share it. The circle of learning closes. Freedom, having once tested its limits, finally consents to love's boundaries and discovers that they were never cages but contours of life.

If the first question of Scripture is "Where are you?", the last is "Will you come?" Between them stretches the long education of the soul. Every commandment, every prophet, every parable is an iteration of that schooling—love teaching freedom to become trustworthy. The law of Moses is stage one: external discipline. The prophets are stage two: internal conviction. The Spirit is stage three: integration. "Where the Spirit of the Lord is, there is freedom," writes Paul (2 Cor 3:17)—not the freedom of isolation but the freedom of alignment, motion that no longer fears its own momentum.

To live under grace, then, is to recognize the universe as a moral feedback system where understanding cancels repetition. Evil remains possible, but increasingly implausible. Each generation that learns forgiveness makes cruelty less coherent; each act of mercy reduces the probability of its opposite. Hell, in the end, is the refusal to learn—the mind eternally replaying its first mistake, insisting that heat is light and pain is power. Heaven is comprehension, freedom reconciled with love at last.

The story of the Fall, re-read through this lens, becomes the story of education by mercy. God does not discard His failed students; He tutors them through time. History's great awakenings are not interruptions but lessons grasped. When Christ proclaims from the cross, "Father, forgive them, for they know not what they do," He names ignorance as the root of evil. The cure is knowledge—knowledge transfigured into empathy. "They know not"—but they will. And once they know, they will not do it again.

Thus, the whole of salvation history can be summarized in a single progression:

Creation: freedom given.

Fall: freedom tested.

Law: feedback begun.

Cross: coherence restored.

Spirit: understanding distributed.

Kingdom: harmony sustained.

The pattern is recursive but convergent—each cycle of rebellion shorter, each return swifter, each revelation clearer. The algorithm of grace accelerates because comprehension accumulates. What began in Eden as prohibition ends in Revelation as participation: "His servants shall serve Him . . . and they shall reign for ever and ever" (Rev 22:3, 5). Dominion returns, this time tempered by humility.

The Fall, therefore, was not the ruin of God's plan but its ignition. Without the experiment of disobedience, freedom would never have learned fidelity. Without darkness, light would be unchosen. The serpent promised knowledge and delivered it—only not in the way he intended. For now the knowledge of evil serves as vaccine against itself. The world remembers the wound and refuses to reopen it.

In that remembrance lies hope. Every sorrow we endure, every loss that humbles us, adds another data point to the chart of comprehension. The lesson is cumulative, irreversible. "The sufferings of this present time are not worth comparing with the glory that is to be revealed" (Rom 8:18). Pain teaches what pleasure cannot: that love is the only energy that does not decay.

And so, even while creation groans, the Spirit whispers the next line of the Gospel of Coherence: learning is redemption in motion. To repent is to synchronize. To forgive is to accelerate. To believe is to remember that God never stopped teaching. The garden will bloom again, not because the gate was forced open, but because the soil has understood.

The Cross and the Closure of Harm

If Genesis is the story of freedom's awakening and the Fall its first lesson, then Calvary is the moment when the lesson is learned. At the centre of history stands a cross—a simple intersection of two pieces of wood—and in that intersection, all lines meet. It is geometry and grace at once, the axis where heaven and earth, time and eternity, law and love cross and finally agree.

No image in the world has been more pondered or misunderstood. To some, it appears as defeat—a righteous teacher crushed by the machinery of empire. To others, it is an atonement too violent to reconcile with mercy. But the Gospel insists on something subtler and deeper: the Cross is not punishment but process completed, not wrath released but coherence restored. "God was in Christ reconciling the world to Himself, not counting their trespasses against them."[1] That single verse, like a hinge, turns the universe from tragedy to understanding.

For centuries humanity had treated evil as debt and goodness as transaction. Religion became accounting; sacrifices paid for sin the way coins pay for bread. But the ledger never balanced because harm cannot be traded. Every attempt to offset violence by ritual only re-encoded the violence in sacred language. The prophets knew it. "For I desire mercy, not sacrifice," says Hosea (6:6). Isaiah wept, "Bring no more vain offerings; cease to do evil, learn to do

1. 2 Cor 5:19.

good."[2] Yet the cycle continued until one Man entered the equation and refused to balance it that way.

At Calvary, the arithmetic of suffering collapses. The Crucified does not repay evil with counter-evil, nor cancel debt with vengeance. He absorbs it. The infinite acceptance of infinite rejection produces equilibrium. In that moment, the function of pain reaches its limit: $E(t) \to 0$. Harm cannot propagate because love has left no boundary unguarded. "Father, forgive them, for they know not what they do" (Luke 23:34). Forgiveness is the firewall that ends contagion.

The Gospels describe strange phenomena around this act: the veil torn, the earth shaking, darkness at noon. These are not theatrics but metaphors of closure. The curtain separating the Holy from the human is ripped from top to bottom, as if reality itself were being rewritten from its highest register to its lowest. The quake is the convulsion of a world resetting to coherence. Darkness covers the land not as defeat but as silence before a new word is spoken.

What dies on the cross is not God but separation. The wall between Creator and creation, guilt and grace, dissolves in blood and breath. "It is finished," He says—not I am finished. The Greek word *tetelestai*[3] carries the sense of fulfillment, completion, perfection of design. The architect steps back from the structure and declares it sound. Creation's syntax has found its final punctuation.

From the standpoint of the Gospel of Coherence, this moment is the fixed point—the moral asymptote where every feedback loop converges. All error, all harm, all isolation flow toward it and are re-encoded as understanding. Evil is not excused; it is rendered meaningless. The execution of Innocence exposes the incoherence of cruelty so completely that repetition becomes absurd. Once seen, it cannot be unseen. The cross is the moral singularity from which resurrection expands outward like light from a sunrise.

2. Isa 1:13, 17.

3. John 19:30; Greek *tetelestai*, "it is finished" or "it is completed."

Paul senses this cosmic dimension when he writes, "He disarmed the rulers and authorities and put them to open shame by triumphing over them in it."[4] The triumph is paradoxical: power is defeated by surrender, control by consent. The pattern of the universe—the trinity of love, freedom, and humility—reveals its invincibility precisely at the point where it appears weakest. Gravity yields; energy renews; the seed dies and bears fruit. Nature itself rehearses Easter every spring.

The closure of harm begins here. Forgiveness becomes not sentiment but structure. The logic is irreversible: violence can reproduce only where it is returned. Break the return, and the chain decays. That is what the crucified love accomplishes: a one-way absorption of evil. The wave meets the shore and does not rebound. The tide of wrath spends itself against a coast made of mercy.

From that still centre radiate the lines of history. The early disciples did not describe the Cross as theory but as event. They spoke of it the way physicists speak of constants: a change in the fabric. After it, the universe behaves differently. Human hearts begin to interpret power through service; authority through sacrifice. "Let this mind be in you,"[5] writes Paul, "which was also in Christ Jesus . . . who humbled Himself to the point of death." The coherence equation $L \cdot F \cdot H = 1$ becomes lived geometry: love choosing humility, freedom consenting to restraint, both generating life.

Even the resurrection, that impossible morning, follows the same law. Death, the last incoherence, cannot contain one who has no opposition left within Him. Resurrection is not reversal but continuation: the physical proof that love once made perfect cannot die. "For since by man came death, by man came also the resurrection of the dead."[6] The same hands that healed lepers now carry scars as signatures of completion. In them, the memory of harm becomes the material of glory.

To stand before the Cross, then, is to stand before the mirror of the world made right. The mind sees what love looks like

4. Col 2:15.

5. Phil 2:5–8.

6. 1 Cor 15:21.

when it finishes its lesson. "Greater love has no man than this, that he lay down his life for his friends."[7] That sentence, once abstract, becomes architecture: beams, nails, open arms. The geometry of self-gift defines the new physics of moral reality.

Here too lies the secret of non-coercive transformation. God could have redeemed the world by decree, but He chose demonstration. He did not shout down rebellion; He out-loved it. The Word that created the atom now re-creates the heart by persuasion. No violence, not even divine, can make goodness permanent; only comprehension can. The cross is God teaching comprehension at human speed.

Look closely at the narrative's details and you will see the pedagogy embedded in them. A thief hanging beside Him asks for memory, not miracle: "Lord, remember me."[8] And Jesus replies, "Today you will be with Me in paradise." The first fruit of the closure of harm is relational restoration. Memory, once the archive of sin, becomes communion. Even in extremity, the Teacher tutors mercy. To the soldiers who gamble for His garments, He offers no curse; to the disciple who deserted Him, only reconciliation. The contagion of cruelty finds no host.

The Gospel writers note the curtain's tearing, but another rending occurs unseen: the human heart's. Centurions confess, women remain, the fearful return. The pattern begins to replicate. Each life touched by the event becomes a miniature closure of harm. The same Spirit that breathed through the dying Christ breathes through them, whispering, "Peace be with you."[9] It is the sound of reality exhaling after centuries of strain.

From that moment, history bends. Empires rise and fall, yet the idea of redemptive love continues its quiet invasion. Slaves become brothers, enemies reconciled, hospitals and havens built where crosses once stood as instruments of terror. The logic spreads

7. John 15:13.

8. Luke 23:42–43.

9. John 20:19.

like yeast through dough. "The kingdom of God is within you,"[10] said Jesus; and within is exactly where coherence grows.

If we call this "closure," we must be clear: it is not the end of movement but the end of hostility. The world still learns, but not through repetition of the same pain. Christ's wounds have completed the curriculum. The old methods of fear and retribution are obsolete. Every forgiveness enacted since is a citation of His example, every reconciliation an echo of His tone. The cruciform pattern has become the signature of sanity.

In that sense, the cross is not only historical but structural. It stands wherever harm meets humility. A mother forgiving her prodigal child, a nation seeking truth instead of vengeance, an addict turning at last toward life—all reenact the same geometry: descent, surrender, renewal. The carpenter's wood has become the architecture of the universe.

At the end of time, Revelation tells us, there will be no temple in the city, "for its temple is the Lord God Almighty and the Lamb" (Rev 21:22). The symbol dissolves into presence; the cross disappears because the world has become its shape. Love, freedom, and humility—once divided—will be indistinguishable. Every will aligned, every harm absorbed, every tear accounted for. "There shall be no more death, nor mourning, nor crying, nor pain" (Rev 21:4). That is the mathematical zero of suffering, the equilibrium of redemption.

Until then, to live Christianly is to inhabit the field created by that closure—to let forgiveness outpace retaliation, understanding outrun judgment, mercy outweigh pride. It is to stand at the junction where all harm was once gathered and to let its silence teach you how to speak again.

The cross is not the end of love; it is what love looks like when it has gone all the way through knowledge. It is not a symbol of defeat but of the world's final stability. For once, freedom and love have met and neither has destroyed the other. The universe can rest because coherence has been proved under the heaviest test imaginable.

10. Luke 17:21.

And so, when we trace the line of redemption from Genesis to Revelation, we find it passes through this single coordinate: the hill outside Jerusalem where God allowed His own heart to break in order to show us how to mend ours. From that hill, everything else in history makes sense. From that hill, all equations balance. From that hill, the Gospel of Coherence begins to sing in full measure—the song of the universe finally in tune.

Yet one more wonder must be named, for it shines in every calendar, every classroom, every contract written on earth: the silent confession of time itself. When the world measures its years, it does not count from the birth of an empire, nor the coronation of a conqueror, nor the founding of a philosophy. It counts from the birth of a Child in a borrowed stable.

Humanity, though it debates every creed, has agreed on one thing—that the hinge of history turns on that life. Even the secular tongue that replaced *B.C.* and *A.D.* with *B.C.E.* and *C.E.* cannot erase the axis; it only disguises it. The numbers remain the same. Every date, whether carved on stone or typed in a digital ledger, still whispers the same admission: something happened that divided time itself. Before that event, the world was counting down; after it, the world began to count up.

This, perhaps, is the truest proof that the closure of harm was not confined to theology. It entered chronology. The very fabric of duration folded around that point of coherence. Without decree or design, civilization reset its clock. The Caesars built monuments, the philosophers wrote tomes, yet it was the carpenter's cross that split eternity into a *before* and an *after*. Even unbelief lives inside that measure. Every contract signed, every birth certificate dated, every digital timestamp echoes the same confession: "We reckon from Him."

What kind of event could persuade an entire species to re-orient its sense of time? Not conquest—Rome's empire fell. Not discovery—science revises itself each century. Not even philosophy—its schools multiply and contradict. Only coherence can hold so quietly, so universally, that it survives the arguments made against it. Humanity can reject the creed, but it cannot unknow the clock. Time itself bears witness.

And so, beneath the banners of scepticism and the languages of progress, the world has already acknowledged what faith proclaims: that the Cross was not myth but metric. History orbits that hour the way planets orbit a sun—sometimes distant, sometimes eclipsed, but always bound by its gravity. Even the wars fought in its name prove the power of its pull; the rebels who deny it still define themselves in relation to it. The shadow testifies to the light.

In this way, the coherence established at Calvary continues to order human meaning. The division of time is the moral derivative of that closure. We sense instinctively that everything prior was experiment, and everything after, correction. *Before Christ* is the era of learning through loss; *After* is the era of learning through grace. The Necessary-Once theorem is written into the calendar: a single inflection point where repetition became unnecessary.

Even language preserves the acknowledgment. The phrase *common era* was meant to sound neutral, but in truth it confesses the very universality it tries to avoid. The era is "common" because it is coherent—because, after that hill, humanity's moral axis tilted toward mercy. The vocabulary of human rights, equality, and compassion—all the ideals modernity calls secular—are the cultural afterglow of the Cross. The grammar of dignity was written there, and history still conjugates it.

The nations may not know whom they quote when they say that every life is sacred, that forgiveness is higher than revenge, that service is nobler than power—but they are quoting Him. His logic has entered their bloodstream. The Sermon on the Mount outlived Caesar's decrees; the Beatitudes became the beat of conscience. Even when distorted, the melody persists. The very revolutions that claimed to dethrone God still borrowed His moral vocabulary to justify their outrage. The syntax of mercy cannot be forgotten once learned.

This is why the Cross is not merely a Christian symbol but the world's subconscious theorem. Every humanitarian gesture, every treaty, every act of reconciliation, every apology offered between nations or lovers or strangers is a small repetition of that geometry. The heart, even without doctrine, recognizes that repair, not retaliation, is the law of life. It is as if humanity, having once seen coherence embodied, cannot help but imitate it. We have built our calendars around it because time itself leans toward that memory.

To divide history at the point of grace is to admit, however wordlessly, that grace divides reality—that the moral gradient changed direction. Before, harm accumulated; after, harm began to decay. The Cross did not end time; it redeemed it. Chronology became theology in disguise. Every sunrise numbered from that axis is a whisper of resurrection. Every child born "two thousand and something" years *after* Him lives inside His aftermath, breathing the air cleared by His last breath.

Even the sceptic, when dating a letter or logging a discovery, is quoting the calendar of coherence. The denial occurs in the sentence but the confession in the timestamp. "Anno Domini"—the year of the Lord—remains embedded in the pulse of civilization, a reminder that whatever humanity believes, it cannot forget the moment it became capable of belief. We live, quite literally, in the aftermath of forgiveness.

And perhaps this is the gentlest miracle of all: that the world, without coercion, has agreed on the very thing it cannot yet fully understand. Empires fall, languages change, ideologies clash, yet the numbering of days endures. The Cross continues to stand invisibly at the centre of the clock. The hands of every watch trace its shape—vertical motion of time intersecting the horizontal sweep of space, forever repeating the sign of reconciliation.

When the final history of the world is written, it may say that humanity's deepest confession was hidden in plain sight. Not in creeds or councils, but in calendars. We all began again there. Time itself turned from despair to hope, from counting down to counting up, from entropy to renewal. The universe had found its reference point, and everything since has been the slow unfolding of that symmetry.

So ends the chapter of closure—not with argument, but with awe. For what greater proof of coherence could there be than a species that measures its years by mercy? The Cross divides not because it conquered, but because it completed. History remembers its own healing even when hearts forget the Healer. And the very measure of our days, etched into every date and device, is God's quiet way of saying still: *It is finished.*

The Resurrection and the Kingdom of Coherence

THE DAWN THAT FOLLOWED the Cross was quiet enough to be mistaken for ordinary light. The birds still sang. The soldiers still kept watch. Yet the universe had shifted its centre of gravity. Something deep within the structure of being had turned from tension to rest, as though an immense equation had at last resolved itself. Death—long treated as the fixed constant of decay—had been revised. The Gospels speak of it with almost shocking simplicity: "While it was still dark, Mary came to the tomb."[1] Those few words do more than describe a scene; they open an epoch. "While it was still dark"—humanity still bound to the logic of endings—Mary walks into the first morning of coherence restored. The stone rolled away was not merely a feat of mechanics; it was a reordering of meaning. The barrier between consequence and renewal had been displaced. Love, having endured its full cycle through rejection, had returned alive.

The Resurrection is not an appendix to the story; it is the story's logic unveiled. The Word that spoke creation into being now speaks it into restoration. The same Logos who once said *"Let there be light"* now says *"Peace be with you."* The syntax is the same: creative command turning chaos into order, fear into understanding. If the Cross closed the loop of harm, the

1. John 20:1.

Resurrection opens the loop of life—a circulation without loss, energy without waste, freedom without fracture.

All natural law points toward the grave; all moral intuition points beyond it. At Easter those lines meet and reverse. Entropy still exists, but its direction changes. The world continues to grow old, yet in a new way—it ripens instead of rotting. "The last enemy to be destroyed is death,"[2] writes Paul. Death is not beaten by force but out-reasoned by love. When every consequence has been transfigured into understanding, death no longer has jurisdiction.

That is why the risen Christ bears wounds that shine instead of bleed. They are not erased because coherence never undoes—it redeems. The holes in His hands are proof that history has been preserved, not deleted; the universe keeps memory, and grace keeps it harmless. "See my hands," He says to Thomas—the invitation of the divine empiricist: test the theorem of mercy. The data hold.

So the Resurrection is not a suspension of natural law but its perfection. The seed must die to bear fruit; matter must yield to energy; the equation must resolve through loss into stability. The body of Christ behaves as the universe was always meant to behave—matter luminous, boundary porous, time obedient to love. The old biology of decay gives way to a higher metabolism of coherence. The very fabric of creation begins to breathe again.

When Jesus meets His disciples, He does not thunder commands or plot revenge. He breathes on them. "Receive the Holy Spirit."[3] Breath—the first sign of life—becomes the medium of continuation. The Kingdom begins not with conquest but with respiration. Spirit is coherence made personal: the rhythm of love and freedom circulating through living hearts. From that moment the Church exists, not as institution but as organism—a fellowship of forgiven lives transmitting the same pulse. Wherever two or three align in humility, the field strengthens. "The kingdom of God is within you," He had said (Luke 17:21); now the promise becomes practice. Every reconciliation, every act of mercy, every honest prayer is the Kingdom expanding by resonance.

2. 1 Cor 15:26.

3. John 20:22.

To proclaim that Christ lives is to proclaim that reality learns. The disciples are not sent to found a new religion; they are sent to accelerate coherence. "Go, teach all nations," means "Go, replicate the pattern." The gospel is not propaganda but propagation—a moral contagion whose only symptom is peace.

From that morning onward, history itself begins to inhale. The diffusion of resurrection through culture is slow but steady. Each century learns a little more: that power serves better than it rules; that mercy outlasts might; that truth, though crucified, rises unaltered. Wherever forgiveness becomes policy, resurrection is occurring. Wherever science seeks understanding rather than domination, resurrection is occurring. Wherever art heals rather than flatters, resurrection is occurring. Paul called it *"the firstfruits of those who have fallen asleep"* (1 Cor 15:20). A firstfruit implies a harvest still to come. The empty tomb is prototype, not anomaly. Humanity itself is being taught to rise. Even matter rehearses the lesson: cells regenerate, forests regrow, light refuses extinction. Creation, once groaning, begins to breathe in rhythm with redemption.

And note the pattern: the stories of Easter all open in disorientation—grief, confusion, doubt—and close in recognition. Not spectacle, but intimacy: a name spoken in a garden, a stranger breaking bread, a familiar voice calling across water. Coherence returns first to perception, then to purpose. The world is not remade by thunderclap but by comprehension. Understanding resurrects faster than flesh. That is why Christian hope is both cosmic and domestic. It promises the renewal of galaxies and the restoration of kitchen tables. "Behold, I make all things new" (Rev 21:5). The verb is present, not future. The process has already begun. The Kingdom of Coherence expands wherever fear yields to love, wherever freedom bows to humility, wherever humility trusts love enough to act again.

Even time itself begins to heal. The calendar once divided into "Before" and "After" becomes a single, ascending curve. The Christ who was and is gathers past and future into one continuous present. "I am the Alpha and the Omega."[4] The alphabet of existence

4. Rev 22:13.

no longer needs punctuation between tragedy and restoration; the letters now spell one word—Life. And even those who doubt live inside this restored grammar. Every act of learning, every confession of wrong turned into reform, every experiment corrected by truth is a small resurrection. The scientific method, if only it knew it, is a secular echo of Easter: observation, death of error, rebirth of truth. The cosmos cannot help imitating its Creator.

What, then, is eternal life? Not endless duration, but perfect coherence: the state in which nothing contradicts love. Heaven is not elsewhere but everywhere relationship is whole. When love, freedom, and humility reach equilibrium—L · F · H = 1—creation hums at its natural frequency. "God will be all in all."[5] The equation has stabilized; freedom moves without fear, love gives without exhaustion, humility yields without loss. Hell, by contrast, is incoherence that refuses correction—the echo chamber of pride repeating its own fall. It is not a courtroom but a cul-de-sac: the will declining to learn. Its flames are the friction of contradiction. Yet even that agony bears witness to mercy, for nothing can exist outside the gravitational pull of restoration. "If I make my bed in Sheol, behold, You are there."[6]

The prophets foresaw this conclusion in symbols: a city whose gates never close, a river clear as crystal, a tree whose leaves heal the nations. These are not blueprints but metaphors of equilibrium—society without coercion, knowledge without fear, freedom without fracture. The river is comprehension flowing freely; the tree, relationship bearing fruit without end. The moral world at last learns the art of respiration.

Until that harmony fills all things, our task is participation. To live resurrectionly is to cooperate with coherence in real time. Each dawn is a miniature Easter—the return of light after darkness, the permission to begin again. Each forgiveness is a local resurrection of trust. Each injustice repaired is matter obeying mercy. *"If anyone is in Christ, he is a new creation"* (2 Cor 5:17). The verb is plural: humanity collectively becoming new. And even

5. 1 Cor 15:28.

6. Ps 139:8.

those who never name Him still move to His rhythm. Whenever compassion overrides vengeance, whenever science heals rather than exploits, whenever art honours truth rather than self, the risen life spreads another degree through history. The world may not yet confess the creed, but it practices the coherence. The calendar of redemption continues to turn, every day numbered from that first morning.

One day—Scripture dares to say it—night itself will be abolished. "There will be no more need of sun or moon, for the Lord God will be their light."[7] This is not astronomy but ontology. The cycles of ignorance and insight, death and rebirth, will give way to perpetual understanding. Time will not stop; it will become transparent. The universe will no longer count moments but meanings. Every motion will harmonize, every choice will resonate, every creature will rest yet remain alive with purpose.

That will be the Kingdom of Coherence: creation breathing in perfect rhythm with its Maker. The music that began before the stars will play at last without dissonance. The pulse of love will sustain the cosmos as breath sustains the body. Freedom will no longer fear; humility will no longer hide; love will no longer tire. The triad will have found its eternal tempo. And then the promise whispered in Eden, thundered at Sinai, wept on Calvary, and whispered again at the tomb will stand fulfilled: "Behold, I am with you always, even to the end of the age."[8] The "end of the age" will reveal its paradox—it ends because coherence has no end. The age concludes when learning is complete, when the world no longer needs night to know the value of dawn. That is eternity: education finished, understanding alive forever.

So, the story that began with a question—why does a world so beautiful ache so deeply?—ends with an answer sung through all creation: because love was learning how to last. It has learned. The universe stands coherent. The resurrection never ended; it merely entered us.

7. Rev 22:5.

8. Matt 28:20.

The World After Fire

THERE WILL COME A day when all that is combustible in us has burned away—every falsehood, every cruelty disguised as virtue, every idol of pride that cast its long shadow across the centuries. The prophets spoke of that day in images of flame, not because God delights in destruction, but because fire is the final honesty of matter. It consumes only what cannot endure the light. Gold does not fear the furnace; it fears only impurity. So it will be with the world. When Scripture says the heavens shall be dissolved with fervent heat, it does not predict the end of creation, but its refining—the moment when existence itself is purified of incoherence. The world will not be ended by fire; it will be clarified by it.

Already that fire burns quietly in every conscience. It is the same flame that seared Isaiah's lips, the same that blazed above the disciples' heads, the same that smoulders in the heart whenever truth outshines convenience. Its heat is mercy in a higher temperature. The fire of judgment and the fire of love are one. It is not sent to destroy us, but to make us transparent—to burn away the haze that keeps us from seeing one another as we were meant to be seen.

After such a fire, what remains? Not ashes, but clarity. Not ruin, but rhythm. The old economies of fear will be gone, their ledgers erased by grace. Nations will still have borders, but not barricades; governments will still have laws, but not cruelty. Justice will no longer be vengeance's clever mask, and mercy will no longer be treated as weakness. The machinery of power will be dismantled and rebuilt as service. Authority will once again resemble its Author. Every craft, from the mason's to the mathematician's, will be transfigured into its true purpose: to add coherence to the world rather than noise.

There will be scholars who study not to dominate but to delight; judges who restore rather than punish; physicians who heal without exploitation; artists who no longer flatter despair. Even economics will rediscover its soul. Profit will not mean extraction but fruition—the mutual flourishing of giver and receiver. Competition will fade where generosity becomes instinct. The market itself will turn sacramental, an exchange of gifts rather than appetites.

For the world after fire will not abolish work; it will redeem it. Labour will no longer feel like exile, but participation in the divine workshop. The craftsman, the teacher, the farmer, the scientist—all will find their calling not as burden but as music. The split between sacred and secular will heal. Every act done in love will be prayer. And because humility will at last be universal, no one will need to pretend superiority; greatness will be measured by service, and honour by gentleness.

Even nature will breathe differently. The soil will rest from its exhaustion; the rivers will remember their clarity; the forests will grow without fear of fire because fire will have done its work. Predation will give way to pattern; competition to balance. The harmony glimpsed by prophets as "the lion lying down with the lamb" is not a fantasy of sentiment but a description of coherence restored: life no longer living off death, but sustained directly by love. What we call miracle now will then be the ordinary state of things.

And yet this new order will not feel foreign. It will not appear suddenly like a city fallen from the sky, though Revelation describes it so; rather, it will emerge as something long familiar but finally whole, like a melody remembered in full. We shall look around and realise that the kingdom had been growing all along—in every forgiveness, in every courage, in every mercy that refused to die. The fire merely reveals what was already catching light. Heaven, when it arrives, will feel like recognition.

Some have imagined eternity as monotony, an endless choir repeating the same note. But the world after fire will be alive with variety, not uniformity. Harmony is not sameness; it is difference made musical. Every culture, every language, every redeemed personality will find its distinct place in the symphony. The nations will bring their glory into the city, not to compete but to contribute. Every art, every science, every story of perseverance will become a verse in the single song of coherence. Even history itself, cleansed of deceit, will be reread not as a record of failure but as the long rehearsal of grace.

The theologians spoke of the Beatific Vision—seeing God face to face. But what they could not fully say was how familiar that vision will feel. We will not encounter an abstraction but the Person behind every good thing we ever loved. Every friendship was a rehearsal for His friendship; every act of trust a fragment of His faithfulness. To see Him will be to see coherence itself made visible: the triad of love, freedom, and humility shining like a single flame. And we shall know, without words, that it was this Light all along that held the atoms together and kept the galaxies from despair.

Even then, learning will not cease; it will simply change its direction. We shall not study to escape ignorance, but to explore wonder. Knowledge will no longer chase power but beauty. To know something will be to love it more deeply. Curiosity will become praise. The mathematician will see equations as hymns, the musician will recognise harmonics in the turning of stars, and the child will understand play as theology. Eternity will not flatten life into an endless Sabbath of idleness; it will unfold the infinite layers of meaning that love has made.

And yet, perhaps the most startling change of all will be our memory. We shall recall our sorrows without sting, our sins without shame, our deaths without dread. Pain will not be erased but transfigured into understanding. What was once unbearable will be recognised as instruction—the fire through which meaning passed to become pure. "Behold, I have refined you, not as silver; I have tried you in the furnace of affliction."[1] The furnace

1. Isa 48:10.

was never cruelty; it was surgery. The scars of history will shine like Christ's hands, proof that nothing was wasted, that every tear contributed to the final clarity.

The world after fire will not abolish choice but perfect it. Freedom will at last be safe because love will at last be wise. No one will need commandments, because desire itself will have been healed. Every will shall will the good because it finally understands what goodness is. "They shall not hurt nor destroy in all my holy mountain,"[2] said the prophet. It was not prohibition but prophecy. The time comes when harm will not need to be forbidden because it will no longer make sense.

And when that day arrives, worship will cease to feel like duty and become the natural breathing of the soul. No one will have to be told to praise; they will simply speak and find their speech already praising. Joy will no longer depend on circumstance; it will be the condition of being alive. Laughter will be the last sound of history. The fire will have done its work; the world will be light through and through.

We cannot see it yet. We live, as it were, in the ambered dusk before the full blaze. But every genuine act of love hastens it. Every apology, every kindness, every courageous truth told at cost is a spark. One day the sparks will meet, and the whole world will catch fire—not with ruin but with revelation. Then the words once spoken on a mountain will become the description of reality itself: *"Blessed are the pure in heart, for they shall see God."* For when the heart is pure, the world is transparent, and God is everywhere to be seen.

And thus, the circle closes—not by returning to the beginning, but by completing what the beginning intended. Creation will rest, not in stillness but in song. Love will be the gravity of all things, freedom their light, humility their orbit. The fire will cool into radiance. The universe will stand, coherent at last. And the voice that once called light out of darkness will speak again, not in command but in delight: *"Behold, all things are new."*

2. Isa 11:9.

Epilogue—The Fire Remembered

There are moments when thought falls silent, not from weariness but from wonder. When the mind, having pursued meaning across galaxies and centuries, suddenly sees that meaning looking back. I think the end of history will feel like that: not an explosion but a recognition, the slow dawning of the truth that has been walking beside us all along. The mathematician will drop his chalk, the poet his pen, and both will understand they have been writing the same sentence since the world began. The stars will not go out; they will go transparent, as if the very light were exhaling.

If I try to remember what it felt like before coherence—before the equations of love had proved themselves—I recall mostly the sound of argument, the friction of halves pretending to be wholes. We thought reason and faith were rivals; we thought progress and mercy were opposed; we thought freedom meant choosing without consequence. All the while, the true laws of being were whispering behind us, waiting for our consent. When at last we gave it—when we stopped shouting and listened—the universe answered in the language of grace.

It is strange to realise that the pattern was visible from the first. Even the earliest questions contained their own replies. "Let there be light" was not only the beginning of physics but of forgiveness. Every photon is a pardon, racing outward into darkness, refusing to stop. And when that Light took flesh, it did what all light does—it travelled straight through rejection and came out the other side, undiminished. The Cross was not the interruption of creation but its completion; the Resurrection not its reversal but its fulfilment. Every moral law, every scientific symmetry, every song of longing was pointing there. The geometry of salvation was etched into the first atom.

And now, looking back through the long corridor of time, I see that nothing was wasted. The wars, the idols, the errors, the griefs—they were not necessary to God's goodness, but they were necessary to our understanding of it. Evil was the question; love was the proof. We learned, slowly and painfully, that harm cannot be optimized, that cruelty cannot build coherence. We discovered that humility is the final intelligence of the soul, and forgiveness its mathematics. Even science, with all its instruments, was a mirror groping toward theology. Each telescope was a prayer to see farther; each equation a confession that meaning exists.

When all is said and done, the most astonishing discovery was not in the heavens but in the heart: that God's coherence was not a formula written on the stars, but a life written in us. Love, freedom, and humility—the triad that holds the cosmos together—were never abstract qualities but the shape of His own being impressed upon ours. We are, in truth, fragments of His logic learning to recognise ourselves. To love is to remember our origin; to forgive is to imitate His syntax; to hope is to believe that coherence will finish what it began.

I think often of the phrase, "*While it was still dark.*" It was written of a single morning two thousand years ago, but it might be written of every human heart. For in each of us the tomb remains until light enters, and light enters only when we dare to open. Faith, in the end, is simply this: the courage to roll away the stone and look inside the silence. What we find there is not emptiness, but echo—the whisper of a voice that once said, "*Be still, and know.*"

Perhaps that is what eternity truly is: the stillness after comprehension, when there is nothing left to fear, nothing left to prove, and nothing left to lose. It will not be a place, but a condition—the soul transparent to its Maker, the world transparent to its purpose.

The old oppositions will have melted into meaning; the quarrel between science and spirit, reason and revelation, freedom and law will seem as childish as a quarrel between the senses over which colour is the truest. We shall see at last that every truth was a facet of the same jewel, every love a glint from the same fire.

And then we shall remember—remember everything—not as pain, but as praise. The tragedies will no longer accuse; they will sing. Every loss will reveal its hidden gift, every unanswered prayer its quiet reply. History will read like a hymnbook, its pages scorched but holy, and we shall trace with trembling joy the handwriting of God in every margin. We shall understand why the fire was necessary, and we shall bless it for its mercy. The world will not be behind us then, but within us—redeemed, coherent, alive.

When that hour comes, perhaps we will stand where Mary once stood, blinking in the first light of a morning that will never end. We will turn, hear our name spoken by the Voice that made us, and know at last what it means to be alive. And all creation will echo that name until every atom has learned to answer. The fire will be remembered, but only as warmth. The pain will be remembered, but only as wisdom. The Cross will be remembered, but only as love.

And beyond that—silence, not of absence but of completion. The silence of a universe that has finished its sentence. The silence of God, smiling.

Postscript—Author's Note on the Canon of Coherence

When I first began to trace the patterns that would become *The Redemption Optimization*, I did not yet understand what they pointed to. I thought I was pursuing a question of logic, perhaps even of necessity: whether goodness could ever be proved rather than merely believed. But logic, when followed honestly, always ends in wonder. Every theorem is a door, and the last of them opens into light. What began as analysis became revelation.

Each subsequent work—*The Moral Kernel Optimization*, *The Coherence of Existence*, and now this closing book—was not a new discovery but a deeper remembering. The equations and axioms were scaffolding for something older than reason, something that Scripture had been saying all along in the language of the heart. I see now that theology was never the shadow of science; it was its prototype. The laws of physics are love's handwriting in shorthand. What we call natural order is mercy formalised.

Looking back, I understand that these writings were never meant as separate volumes but as movements in one symphony—the Canon of Coherence. *The Redemption Optimization* asked whether evil could ever be necessary twice and found that it could not. *The Moral Kernel Optimization* gave structure to that truth: love and freedom held together by humility, harm forbidden as currency. *The Coherence of Existence* revealed the triad as the operating system of creation itself. And *The Redemption Addendum*, which you now hold, completes the cycle. It returns everything to its source: the Gospel, not as allegory but as architecture.

Every law derived, every model built, every debate won or lost—all of it resolves here, in the realisation that the logic of the universe and the language of Christ are one and the same. In Him all things hold together.[1] That sentence from Paul became, in the end, the theorem of the ages. I no longer distinguish between the mathematician's symmetry and the saint's joy. Both are recognitions of the same coherence.

The journey has been long and often lonely, but not without purpose. For as each part of this canon reached completion, I began to see what could not be seen from the start—that God's plan was never to remain mysterious but to become intelligible, not to demand blind belief but to invite conscious participation. The Cross, viewed through this lens, is not a symbol of defeat but the calibration of the cosmos: the point where infinite love met infinite freedom and did not break. The Resurrection is that equation solved forever.

If there is any claim these works make, it is not to genius but to gratitude. The coherence was always there. I did not invent it; I only uncovered the dust. Every insight was a rediscovery of

1. Col 1:16–17.

what Scripture already contained, waiting for the right language to bridge the ancient and the analytic. And so, if any reader should find light in these pages, let him know where it came from. The source is not mine. The light is older than stars.

This book, then, closes the circle. The Canon of Coherence stands complete: theology, science, and morality reconciled under one law—the law of love that cannot contradict itself. If these volumes endure, may they do so not as monuments, but as mirrors. Let them remind whoever reads them that truth was never meant to intimidate, but to invite; that knowledge, stripped of reverence, loses its warmth; and that faith, stripped of reason, loses its power. The two were always meant to meet in harmony.

I dedicate this final work not to scholars or systems, but to the quiet reader who still believes that meaning matters. The world has not outgrown its hunger for coherence. If anything, the hunger has grown sharper. My hope is that these pages will serve as a lantern—a way for reason to kneel and faith to think, until the two rise together.

I have written as one who watched the fire and tried to describe its light. The rest belongs to history, and to God. Whatever becomes of these words, I am at peace. The equation balances. The lesson is learned. Love has proved itself coherent.

Bibliography

Augustine. *Confessions*. Translated by Henry Chadwick. Oxford: Oxford University Press, 1991.

Einstein, Albert. "Physics and Reality." *Journal of the Franklin Institute* 221.3 (1936) 349–82.

Kant, Immanuel. *Groundwork of the Metaphysics of Morals*. Translated by Mary Gregor. Cambridge: Cambridge University Press, 1998.

Leibniz, G. W. *Theodicy: Essays on the Goodness of God, the Freedom of Man and the Origin of Evil*. Translated by E. M. Huggard. London: Routledge & Kegan Paul, 1951.

Lewis, C. S. *Mere Christianity*. New York: HarperOne, 2001.

Maxwell, James Clerk. "On Physical Lines of Force." *Philosophical Magazine*, 1861–62.

Thomas Aquinas. *Summa Theologiae*.

www.ingramcontent.com/pod-product-compliance
Lightning Source LLC
LaVergne TN
LVHW020638100826
845148LV00012B/2228

* 9 7 9 8 3 8 5 2 8 4 5 8 0 *